Best of P9-APD-586

God Is With Us

*Heartwarming Devotions from
the Life of John Wesley*

Nick Harrison

wph wesleyan
publishing
house

Indianapolis, Indiana

Copyright © 2005 by Wesleyan Publishing House
Published by Wesleyan Publishing House
Indianapolis, Indiana 46250
Printed in the United States of America

ISBN-10: 0-89827-317-X
ISBN-13: 978-0-89827-317-5

Library of Congress Cataloging-in-Publication Data

Harrison, Nick.
  Best of all, god is with us : heartwarming devotions from the life of John Wesley /
Nick Harrison.-- 1st ed.
    p. cm.
  ISBN-13: 978-0-89827-317-5 (pbk.)
  ISBN-10: 0-89827-317-X (pbk.)
  1. Devotional literature. 2. Wesley, John, 1703-1791. I. Title.
  BV4832.3.H36 2005
  242--dc22
                                    2005025204

This book is for Beverly,
the most Christian woman I have ever known;
for a truly great Mom, Patricia Harrison;
and for my dearest Methodist friend, Elinor McGee

Acknowledgements

Thanks to Larry Wilson and the wonderful people at Wesleyan Publishing House. They made this book possible. Thanks also to Jim Watkins for his excellent editorial skills, and to Dr. Clarence Bence, of Indiana Wesleyan University, for his helpful advice.

Introductory Note
About John Wesley

What a remarkable man was our brother in Christ, John Wesley! A brief look at his busy life can leave one exhausted and feeling very useless in comparison. After all, the great man lived a full eighty-seven years and was ministering until the very end. Wesley had a constitution of iron. He was always on the go, rarely sick, had no use for leisure time, and left in his wake a movement that, more than two centuries after his death, has influenced tens of millions of Christians worldwide. What an amazing legacy!

Born in Epworth, Lincolnshire, England on June 17, 1703, John Benjamin Wesley was the fifteenth child and second son born to Reverend Samuel Wesley and his devout wife, Susanna. His childhood was notable for the piety and seriousness of the Wesley household. Susanna homeschooled the Wesley children in their earliest years, and then the boys were sent to a boarding school at about age ten.

During those early years at home, Susanna, who was a loving but no-nonsense woman, was determined to raise children who would bring glory to God. Oh, there was laughter and fun in the Wesley household to be sure, but above all else, the children were set on a course designed to result in godly living.

The first major event in the life of the young John was the parsonage fire from which he was dramatically rescued at age five. Forever after, he would refer to himself as "a brand plucked from the burning fire."

After his boarding school education, the young man, John Wesley, entered Oxford, where he was elected a fellow in 1726, qualifying him to teach students in the undergraduate programs. For a brief time, he returned to Epworth, where, as curate, he assisted his father in ministry. This was to be his only experience in a parish, in what we would call pastoral ministry today.

He next returned to his teaching post at Oxford, joining his brother, Charles, and a young aspiring churchman, George Whitefield, in evening sessions to study the Bible and pray. The seriousness of the young men soon brought derision from their peers, who dubbed the group "the Holy Club." During this time, the "Methodist" label also took hold in reference to the group's "strict conformity to the method of study prescribed by the university." The term Methodist derived from the scholastic study typical in the late middle ages of medieval universities requiring great rigor and discipline on one's academic and devotional life.

In 1735, John, Charles, and two others from the Holy Club set sail for the American colony of Georgia to serve as missionaries to the Native Americans. En route, a storm tossed the ship and John feared that he would perish. With great surprise he observed several other passengers—Moravian believers—whose faith, during the tempests, kept fear at bay by an inner confidence in the power and grace of God.

Wesley's two-year sojourn in Georgia was largely a failure, and the defeated young man sailed home to England. Behind him, he left a shattered romance and rejection both from the English colonists who had no use for his high church ways and the Native Americans with whom Wesley had made no progress.

Out of this bitter disappointment, John turned the critical corner that led to his earth-shaking fifty-five-year ministry. At this point, at the end of himself, he wrote in his journal on January 24, 1738:

> I went to America to convert the Indians, but, O! who shall convert me? who, what is he that will deliver me from this evil heart of unbelief ? I have a fair summer religion; I can talk well, nay, and believe myself, while no danger is near; but let death look me in the face, and my spirit is troubled. Nor can I say, to die is gain. . . . I show my faith by my works, by staking my all upon it. I would do so again and again a thousand times, if the choice were still to make. Whoever sees me sees I would be a Christian. . . . But in a storm I think, What if the Gospel be not true ? . . . O who will deliver me from this fear of death? . . . Where shall I fly from it?

The answer was near. Back in London, Wesley met Peter Bohler, a Moravian, who led him to an understanding of salvation by faith. A short time later he attended a meeting of the Moravians, which led him to record the most oft-quoted passage from his lifelong journal. On May 24, 1738, he wrote:

> In the evening I went very unwillingly to a society in Aldersgate Street, where one was reading Luther's preface to the Epistle to the Romans. About a quarter before nine, while he was describing the change which God works in the heart through faith in Christ, I felt my heart strangely warmed. I felt I did trust in Christ, Christ alone, for salvation; and an assurance was given me that He had taken away my sins, even mine, and saved me from the law of sin and death. I began to pray with all my might for those who had in a more especial

manner despitefully used me and persecuted me. I then testi-
fied openly to all there what I now first felt in my heart.

By that September both John and Charles were preaching the
gospel that had warmed their hearts wherever they could. For many of
the traditional Anglican churches, the message appeared too common,
too basic, for the higher church sensibilities that prevailed. More and
more the church doors were closed to their ministry, and the brothers
were limited to preaching to the small religious societies that were
popular at that time.

The following year, 1739, John Wesley did what he had previous-
ly regarded as far too demeaning. He followed his old friend George
Whitefield's example and began preaching to crowds in the open
fields. The doorway opened for what would occupy John Wesley for
the next half century: traveling and preaching. The Methodist revival
was underway.

Wesley labored tirelessly, working rings around men half his age.
He would eventually travel nearly a quarter of a million miles and
preach forty-two thousand sermons, often beginning at five o'clock in
the morning.

His amazing work could not have been accomplished by a man
with a weak constitution. He was rarely sick, claimed to be rarely
tired—despite an extremely rigorous schedule—and was able to sleep
anywhere. Wesley knew from where his strength came. He attributed
his well-being to God's power, his adaptability under adverse circumstances, his habit of rising early each morning (he preached every
morning at five o'clock for more than fifty years and his normal hour
for retiring, when he wasn't delayed by evening preaching, was nine
o'clock—so he did get a full night's sleep, despite his early rising) and
to his "evenness of temper." Wesley was able to let the worry, the grief,
and the railing against him to deflect like water on a duck's back.

Wesley's strong constitution also allowed him to persevere against strong opposition. Not only did the churches refuse him, but whole towns would turn out to run him out of town, often with violence. A great irony was the rejection he experienced when he returned to Epworth to preach at his father's old parish. Refusing to be denied at home, Wesley preached standing on his father's headstone in the Epworth churchyard for eight nights to huge crowds of responsive listeners. Shortly thereafter, he returned to London to share his success with his dying mother who rejoiced to see the revival she and Samuel had prayed for all those years ago.

The inability of Wesley and his followers to preach from the Church of England pulpits resulted in the genesis of the itinerant preacher who would travel the circuit, preaching for a while and then moving on. It would be largely through this unconventional method that the movement spread farther and faster.

An additional complication for Wesley was his personal life. He was once more rebuffed in love, and then, against the advice of those closest to him, including Charles, married Mary, a wealthy widow who would be the thorn in his flesh for three decades. So poorly did they get along, that eventually the couple parted and didn't see each other for the last ten years of Mary's life.

Wesley wrote extensively, including books on various non-religious topics. His output included 233 books, one of which—his medical handbook, *Primitive Physick*—went through twenty-three editions in his lifetime and was a bestseller of the time.

As his extraordinary life drew to a close, Wesley—now eighty-six years old—preached one hundred sermons in sixty towns in just over two months. Finally, on February 23, 1791, John Wesley preached his final sermon in Kingston House in the village of Leatherhead. The text was "Seek ye the LORD while he may be found; call ye upon him while he is near," (Isa. 55:6, KJV).

A few days later, on March 2, 1791, John Wesley, closed his life with the immortal words, "Best of all, God is with us!" and passed into the presence of His dearly beloved Savior. At the time of his death, he was still a member, minister, and lover of his dear Church of England.

John Wesley had never been a man seeking separation from other believers—even from those who opposed him. He often spoke of the unity of all Christians, and sought to maintain communion with others across doctrinal lines. When his friend, George Whitefield had turned to Calvinism and published a tract against Wesley, the latter refused to respond in kind. And in the later years of both men, all was forgiven, and Wesley preached the memorial service for Whitefield who died while on a preaching tour of the American colonies.

Yes, John Wesley is remembered by many for his advancement of doctrines such as Christian perfection, entire sanctification, and the in-filling of the Holy Spirit, but Wesley said that the most important thing he proclaimed was the simple message of justification by faith. It's certain he would much more prefer to be remembered as a man who sought to exalt Christ to the lost and to believers of every stripe.

It's in that spirit that the following ninety devotions are offered. They're not just for Methodists—although surely every Methodist will be blessed by them—but they're also for every follower of Christ. Yes, even the Calvinist, like Wesley's dear friend, George Whitefield. Each devotion is built around a quote or event in Wesley's life that is relevant to us all.

So no matter what your particular persuasion, if you love Christ as John Wesley loved Christ, may each day bring you fresh insight into the God whom our friend John Wesley served so fully.

I

The Inward
Witness

The Spirit Himself bears witness with our spirit
that we are children of God.

—Romans 8:16

John Wesley had two wonderful loving parents: Samuel and Susanna. Both had come from pious families and were determined that their own children would carry on the family heritage of service to God.

But Samuel didn't have an easy life. He constantly battled poverty and misfortune. With a large family, money was always tight and so when disaster struck, it hit the Wesley household hard.

Due to his unpopularity with his own parish, members of Samuel's angry congregation twice set fire to the rectory. Under the strain of mounting debts, Samuel was arrested and sent to Lincoln Jail for four months. Susanna tried to redeem him with her wedding ring, but he refused to allow it. Instead, he made the most of his sentence by ministering to his fellow prisoners.

Yes, his was a hard life. But he prayed for his children and held on tight to God through every misfortune. Shortly before his death, he laid his hand on John's head and prophesied, "The cause of true religion will surely revive in this kingdom." Later, he died while partaking of the Lord's Supper.

Perhaps Samuel's greatest gift to his son was his constant admonition: "The inward witness, son! The inward witness! That is the best evidence of the truth of the Christian religion."

By "the inward witness" Samuel Wesley meant that certain awareness of salvation that passes through the intellect and resides in the heart. It might be called a divine *knowing:* our spirit, that deepest part of our being, bearing witness with God that we are fully *His.*

This inward witness isn't just a one-time experience. Samuel Wesley meant that the best evidence of a true Christian is an *ongoing* experience of the inward witness. Such an intimate experience was what sustained John Wesley through more than half a century of loving and serving God. The inward witness in our spirit, or "testimony of the spirit" as John Wesley called it, will carry us through our entire life as well.

> By the testimony of the Spirit, I mean, an inward impression
> on the soul whereby the Spirit of God immediately and directly
> witnesses to my spirit, that I am a child of God; that Jesus
> Christ hath loved me, and given himself for me; that all my
> sins are blotted out, and I, even I, am reconciled to God.
>
> —from "On Riches"

Every Christian should ejnoy the blessing of this "inward witness." Allow the Spirit of God to show you that you are indeed His. Then learn to live daily by this internal "knowing." To be without it is to be like a child with any certainty of a parent's love.

2

The Fruit
of the Spirit

But the fruit of the Spirit is love, joy, peace, longsuffering,
kindness, goodness, faithfulness, gentleness,
self-control. Against such there is no law.

—Galatians 5:22–23

How do we know that we have the Holy Spirit within? In addition to the vital importance of the "witness of the Spirit," John Wesley also insisted that the fruit of the Spirit be present. Both are necessary for the growing Christian.

> The true witness of the Spirit is known by its fruit, "love, peace, joy;" not indeed preceding, but *following* it. . . . Let none ever presume to rest in any supposed testimony of the Spirit which is separate from the fruit of it.
>
> If the Spirit of God does really testify that we are the children of God, the immediate consequence will be the fruit of the Spirit, even "love, joy, peace, long-suffering, gentleness, goodness, fidelity, meekness, temperance."
>
> And however this fruit may be clouded for a while, during the time of strong temptation, so that it does not appear to the tempted person, while Satan is sifting him as wheat; yet the substantial part of it remains, even under the thickest cloud.

It is true, joy in the Holy Ghost may be withdrawn, during the hour of trial; yea, the soul may be "exceeding sorrowful," while "the hour and power of darkness" continue; but even this is generally restored with increase, till we rejoice "with joy unspeakable and full of glory."

—from "The Witness of the Spirit"

In a Christian, the fruit is there, even though the clouds hide it. The Spirit is there, even though we may go through periods of sorrow. Through all of life, we have the witness of His Spirit and the fruit of the Spirit. They both are our heritage.

And the fruit proves we are of God.

When the witness and the fruit of the Spirit meet together, there can be no longer stronger proof that we are of God.

—from a letter, March 31, 1787

3

The Trouble and Rest of Good Men

There the wicked cease from troubling,
and there the weary are at rest.

—Job 3:17

John Wesley entered the ministry with great hopes, but also with a heart that was not at peace with God. His lack of what might be termed *spiritual fire*, can be seen in the words of what is thought to be the first sermon he wrote: "The Trouble and Rest of Good Men," preached on September 21, 1725. Not surprisingly, the text was from the book of Job.

This was, of course, before Wesley's dramatic "heartwarming" experience at Aldersgate. It was, in fact, just a month before he was to sail for the American colony of Georgia on what would be an ill-fated, but all-important mission for Wesley.

The reader can sense Wesley's spiritual state in the words of this sermon, and though his theology would certainly change in the years ahead, still there is some ore to be mined here.

The whole world is . . . in its present state, only one great infirmary. All that are therein are sick of sin; and their one business there is to be healed. And for this very end, the great

Physician of souls is continually present with them; marking all the diseases of every soul, and "giving medicines to heal its sickness." These medicines are often painful, too: Not that God willingly afflicts His creatures, but He allots them just as much pain as is necessary to their health; and for that reason — because it is so.

In only a few short years, Wesley would become a master nurse for his great healer of souls, the Lord Jesus. And in forming the societies that would take the Methodist message around the world, Wesley would bring healing to millions over the course of the next two hundred plus years.

Years later, Wesley would have this to say:

We may learn . . . what is the proper nature of . . . the religion of Jesus Christ. It is . . . God's method of healing a soul which is thus diseased. Hereby the great Physician of souls applies medicines to heal this sickness; to restore human nature . . . totally corrupted in all its faculties.

God heals all our Atheism by the knowledge of himself, and of Jesus Christ whom He hath sent; by giving us faith, a divine evidence and conviction of God, and of the things of God — in particular, of this important truth, "Christ loved *me*" — and gave himself for *me*."

—from "Original Sin"

4

Reigning
With Him

For if by the one man's offense death reigned through the one,
much more those who receive abundance of grace and of the gift of
righteousness will reign in life through the One, Jesus Christ.

—Romans 5:17

John Wesley sailed for America in 1735 in an effort to bring the
Christian faith to the Native Americans and to minister to the many
colonists who had roots in the Anglican Church. But Wesley was still
in the process of learning how feeble his own faith was and how *he*
was the one who needed to receive ministry.

In the same sentiment did my brother and I remain (with all those
young gentlemen in derision termed *Methodists*) till we
embarked for America, in the latter end of 1735. It was the next
year, while I was at Savannah, that I wrote the following lines:—

> *Is there a thing beneath the sun,*
> *That strives with thee my heart to share?*
> *Ah! tear it thence, and reign alone,*
> *The Lord of every motion there!*

John Wesley's sojourn in Georgia would not be a success. He courted a young woman, fully expecting to make her his wife, only to see her marry another. His mission to the Native Americans of Georgia failed miserably. Wesley was clearly discouraged—and rightly so. It was still nearly three years until he would have his life-changing encounter with God at Aldersgate. And yet, even with his limited faith, Wesley knew that nothing should reign in his heart, except Christ.

We are called to great things. We are not left to be mere pawns of life. We are to *reign* in our current circumstances. "Reign in life," says the apostle Paul. "Through the One, Jesus Christ" (Rom. 5:17).

Heaven will be wonderful—but we don't have to wait until then to reign. We can reign in life *now* by allowing Christ to reign in us.

Let Him reign in you today.

Whosoever will reign with Christ in heaven, must have Christ reigning in him on earth.

—from "A Blow at the Root"

5

A Heart
Strangely Warmed

*Behold, I stand at the door and knock. If anyone hears My voice and
opens the door, I will come in to him and dine with him, and he with Me.
To him who overcomes I will grant to sit with Me on My throne, as
I also overcame and sat down with My Father on His throne.*

—Revelation 3:20–21

The most well-known story in John Wesley's life is his marvelous
"heartwarming" experience at Aldersgate. It was the event from
which all else would flow from the life of Wesley.

> In the evening I went very unwillingly to a society in
> Aldersgate Street, where one was reading Luther's preface
> to the Epistle to the Romans. About a quarter before nine,
> while he was describing the change which God works in
> the heart through faith in Christ, I felt my heart strangely
> warmed. I felt I did trust in Christ, Christ alone for salvation:
> And an assurance was given me, that He had taken away
> *my* sins, even *mine*, and saved *me* from the law of sin and
> death.
>
> —from John Wesley's journal, May 14, 1738

Isn't it remarkable that John Wesley, previous to this occasion,
had been seeking for this very thing? His talks with Peter Bohler had

convinced him that there was more to the Christian life than he had known. And yet this experience eluded him. How like God to open his eyes and heart at a meeting to which Wesley went "unwillingly"!

We have all known God to do the most extraordinary things when we least expect them. We meet a person casually, and not long after, we find we have fallen in love with them. We go to college expecting to embark on one career, only years later, to find ourselves in a much different occupation.

Think about how God has surprisingly directed you to where you are today. Remind yourself of the twists and turns that brought you here.

Then think about where you might be had not your own heart become strangely warmed by His grace—and had God not directed your life precisely as He has.

Give thanks for a heart that has been warmed by God himself. Give thanks that God still warms hearts—and heals them too.

But our comfort is, He that made the heart can heal the heart.

—from a letter, January 14, 1780

6

Draw Me,
Lord

Draw near to God and He will draw near to you.

—James 4:8

t times we all feel distant from God. We search our hearts and find no apparent reason for this seeming estrangement. It's at times like these that we understand what true faith is: It's trusting God in the face of contradictory evidence. It's when your every inclination is to look at your situation and doubt—to ask, "*Why,* God?"

When God told Sarai she was to give birth in her old age, she laughed. When Gideon was told that he had too many soldiers and that he would win the battle if he eliminated all but a few, Gideon was astonished. When Mary was told she would conceive by the Holy Ghost, she asked how this could be. Throughout the Bible, God shows himself strong, *especially* when the circumstances seem impossible.

For John Wesley, his darkest hour of doubt and fear preceded his great breakthrough at Aldersgate where he was surely drawn by God's Spirit, or as he put it, his heart was "strangely warmed." In that gentle night, God was indeed drawing the young Wesley. But what happened in the two years *prior* to Aldersgate? For the young Wesley, it was a time of confusion; a time of literal storms when he wondered if he would survive. But it was through those storms at sea, as he saw the Moravians' faith, that he was drawn to know God in a deeper way.

God often uses storms to draw us. Sometimes He uses sunny weather—we're told in Romans 2:4 that the goodness of God can lead us to repentance.

No matter where we are in our walk with God, He always is employing some divine plan to draw us even closer to himself, to shelter us there. To reveal himself to us beneath His wings. To assure us of His love and care.

If we would have Him draw near in this way—whether in good times or bad—the apostle James's words are especially for us: "Draw near to God and He will draw near to you" (James 4:8).

Draw near by breathing just a prayer of thanksgiving.

He is there.

Oh, thou Saviour of men, save me from trusting in anything but Thee! Draw me after Thee! Let me be emptied of myself, and then fill me with all peace and joy in believing; and let nothing separate me from Thy love in time or in eternity.

—from John Wesley's journal

7

Avoiding Temptation

And do not lead us into temptation, but deliver us from the evil one.

—Matthew 6:13

J ohn Wesley no sooner had his heart strangely warmed at Aldersgate that he faced immediate temptations. In his journal, he records the way he now encountered temptation and the new and more effective way he found to resist it:

> After my return home, I was much buffeted with temptations; but cried out and they fled away. They returned again and again. I as often lifted up my eyes, and He "sent me help from His holy place."

John Wesley was just beginning to understand how to resist the tempter. Only a few days later, he wrote:

> My soul continued in peace, but yet in heaviness because of manifold temptations. I asked Mr. Telchig, the Moravian, what to do. He said, "You must not fight with them as you did

before, but flee from them the moment they appear; and take shelter in the wounds of Jesus."

The very next day, temptation returned to Wesley. His response?

Believing one reason of my want of joy was want of time for prayer, I resolved to do no business till I went to church in the morning, but to continue pouring out my heart before Him. And this day my spirit was enlarged; so that though I was now also greatly tempted, I was more than conqueror, gaining more power thereby to trust and to rejoice in God my Savior.

What, then, do we learn from John Wesley about handling temptations to doubt, fear, or commit sinful acts?

- We naturally expect to fight our temptations, but as Mr. Telchig counsels, we should flee that which tempts us. Do not go where you know temptation awaits.
- Flee to Jesus. Hide in Him.
- Cry out in prayer to God.
- Rejoice in God your savior. Joy repels temptation.

What are your greatest temptations? Where do you find yourself most vulnerable to these sins? Avoid such people and places. Conquering temptation is both a necessity for a growing Christian and a divine right of every child of God. Do not let the Enemy have the upper hand.

You cannot be too careful to keep out of the way of anything that has been the occasion of sin. . . . Do not run yourself into temptation; and God will deliver you from evil.

—from a letter to Dorothy Furly, September 25, 1757

8

The Narrow Gate

Enter ye in at the strait gate: for wide is the gate, and broad is the way,
that leadeth to destruction, and many there be which go in thereat:
Because strait is the gate, and narrow is the way, which leadeth
unto life, and few there be that find it.

—Matthew 7:13–14, KJV

The early Christians were called followers of "the way." And so we are. The way, the gate, to eternal life is necessarily narrow — perhaps uninviting to the natural eye — while the broader road, the one that is more appealing to the natural eye, leads to destruction.

John Wesley, as a lover of men's souls, was not one to mince words when it came to choosing which way to take.

Therefore strive ye now, in this your day, to "enter in at the strait gate." And in order thereto, settle it in your heart, and let it be ever uppermost in your thoughts, that if you are in a broad way, you are in the way that leadeth to destruction.

If many go with you, as sure as God is true, both they and you are going to hell! If you are walking as the generality of men walk, you are walking to the bottomless pit!

Are many wise, many rich, many mighty, or noble traveling with you in the same way? By this token, without going any farther, you know it does not lead to life. Here is a short, a plain, an infallible rule, before you enter into particulars. In whatever profession you are engaged, you must be singular, or be damned! The way to hell has nothing singular in it; but the way to heaven is singularity all over.

If you move but one step towards God, you are not as other men are. But regard not this. It is far better to stand alone, than to fall into the pit. Run, then, with patience the race which is set before thee, though thy companions therein are but few. They will not always be so. Yet a little while, and thou wilt "come to an innumerable company of angels, to the general assembly and Church of the first-born, and to the spirits of just men made perfect."

Today, we who follow the Lord walk on the narrower way. Perhaps our companions are few. Our family and friends do not understand. But we have One who travels the narrow road with us. The rewards of the less traveled road are hidden rewards. They can't be found by looking at the road from afar and wondering. . . . they can only be found as one starts and stays on the narrow journey.

Again, the true way to heaven is a narrow way. Therefore this is another plain sure rule. "They who do not teach men to walk in a narrow way, to be singular, are false prophets."

—from "Upon Our Lord's Sermon on the Mount"

9

Holiness

*Pursue peace with all people, and holiness, without
which no one shall see the Lord.*

—Hebrews 12:14

Before his historic Aldersgate "heartwarming" experience,
Wesley, like most of us, sought to please God by his own good
works—but without success. In his journal entry for May 24, 1738, he
writes:

> Being removed to the university for five years, I still said my
> prayers both in public and private, and read with the Scriptures
> several other books of religion, especially comments on the
> New Testament. Yet I had not all the while so much as a
> notion of inward holiness. . . .

Wesley discovered that praying avidly and reading the Bible were
not the roads to holiness. Rather, as he later discovered they are the
results of holiness. The writer of Hebrews tells us that without holiness
we will not see the Lord. In other places, the Scriptures repeat the
divine command, "Be holy, for I am holy" (1 Pet. 1:16).

What then is the secret to living a holy life?

Clearly, it takes an ongoing experience with the Holy Spirit to enable us to live holy lives. We are holy because we are filled with *His* holiness. The result is that we live holy lives daily. Inward holiness, as a result of the Holy Spirit living within us, is evidenced by outward holiness as we live our daily lives.

But for many of us, it's too easy to go through our day without a conscious reliance on the Holy Spirit to guide us—to live through us—to enable holiness to be seen in us. But when we cultivate the daily habit of acknowledging His presence, we are blessed.

Be holy today. Be filled with the Holy Spirit of God.

But we must love God before we can be holy at all; this being the root of all holiness.

—from "The Witness of the Spirit"

The Eyes of God

The Lord looks down from heaven upon the children of men,
To see if there are any who understand, who seek God.
They have all turned aside,
They have together become corrupt;
There is none who does good,
No, not one.

—Psalm 14:2–3

There are consequences to serving an all-knowing God, Wesley reminds us:

If you believe that God is about your bed, and about your path, and spieth out all your ways, then take care not to do the least thing, not to speak the least word, not to indulge the least thought, which you have reason to think would offend Him.

Suppose that a messenger of God, an angel, be now standing at your right hand, and fixing his eyes upon you, would you not take care to abstain from every word or action that you knew would offend him?

Yea, suppose one of your mortal fellow-servants, suppose only a holy man stood by you, would not you be extremely cautious how you conducted yourself, both in word and action? How much more cautious ought you to be when you know that not a holy man, not an angel of God, but God himself, the Holy One "that inhabiteth eternity," is inspecting your heart, your tongue, your hand, every moment; and that He himself will surely bring you into judgment for all you think, and speak, and act under the sun!

—from "On the Omnipresence of God"

For all practical purposes, sometimes we seem to forget God. We may gossip, think an impure thought, react rudely to someone close to us, or do any other number of foolish things that we wouldn't do if we were fully conscious of God's presence at our side.

Brother Wesley reminds us to be careful of offending God:

If there is not a word in your tongue, not a syllable you speak, but he "knoweth it altogether;" how exact should you be in "setting a watch before your mouth, and in keeping the door of your lips!"

How wary does it behoove you to be in all your conversation; being forewarned by your Judge, that "by your words you shall be justified, or by your words you shall be condemned!"

—from "On the Omnipresence of God"

We can be holy today. We can walk in awareness of God's presence. But we must do it one step at a time. Today, let's pray with the Psalmist: "Set a guard, O Lord, over my mouth; Keep a watch over the door of my lips" (Psalm 141:3).

II

Enemies

The Lord lives!
Blessed be my Rock!
Let the God of my salvation be exalted.
It is God who avenges me,
And subdues the peoples under me;
He delivers me from my enemies.
You also lift me up above those who rise against me;
You have delivered me from the violent man.
Therefore I will give thanks to You, O Lord, among the Gentiles,
And sing praises to Your name.

—Psalm 18:46–49

Do you have enemies? Are there people in your life who despite-fully use you or put obstacles in your path? Someone at work? At home? Maybe even at church?

As John Wesley began preaching his message within the Anglican Church, he soon found himself acquiring enemies with a capital *E*. Churches that once would have welcomed him, now refused him. In his efforts to preach to the small religious societies within the Church, he there again found himself at odds with an increasing number of opponents.

At times, he had whole villages rise up and try to kill him. More than once he barely escaped with his life. And yet Wesley remained cool; so much so that when allowed to speak, he often won over the hearts of his enemies. Men who were ready to kill him one minute offered their brute strength as protection for the evangelist the next minute.

How was this possible? It was because of Wesley's firm trust in His God. Yes, there were enemies, but there was also the God he served—a mighty God, a God who protected Wesley from his enemies.

Like David, Wesley could truthfully say, "You also lift me up above those who rise against me; You have delivered me from the violent man" (Ps. 18:48).

We can say that too. Perhaps we don't have enemies who want to take our life. Perhaps we don't even recognize open enemies that seek to hinder our way. But every Christian has the same ultimate Enemy that Wesley recognized: Satan. Even that fierce Enemy has been overcome by our God.

The truth of the matter is that *no* enemy—even ourselves—can prevail against the God-protected life.

Do you love your enemies? Is your soul full of goodwill, of tender affection toward them? Do you love even the enemies of God, the unthankful and unholy? Does your heart yearn over them? Could you wish yourself temporally accursed for their sake?

—from "A Catholic Spirit"

12

The Danger
of Riches

*For the love of money is a root of all kinds of evil, for which
some have strayed from the faith in their greediness, and
pierced themselves through with many sorrows.*

—1 Timothy 6:10

John Wesley had a fleeting relationship with money. He gave it away almost as soon as he received it. It was his belief that "riches and happiness seldom dwell together." Wesley could have been a very rich man. His bestselling medical books alone could have been a secure source of income. But he would have none of it.

A noted sculptor had been trying to convince Wesley to pose for a bust. Wesley refused until the artist offered him ten guineas, or several day's wages, for a ten-minute sitting.

Wesley accepted the offer and eight minutes into the sitting, the sculptor had "the most perfect bust [he] had ever taken," and immediately paid Wesley the ten guineas. Wesley was quite perplexed by the ease with which he had made the money, saying, "I never till now earned money so speedily; but what shall I do with it?"

But then as Wesley left the man's studio, he came across a woman and her three children who were crying bitterly. Upon inquiry, Wesley discovered that the woman's husband was being sent to prison for a debt of eighteen shillings.

He paid the debt, freeing the husband, and then he continued to Giltspur Street Compter prison where he asked the jailer to show him the most miserable person in his charge. The starving man presented to him was devouring some potato skins. He had been there many months for the debt of a half guinea. Wesley paid the man's debt and gave him an extra half guinea for a new start.

Then another desperate man was presented to him. He sat in the prison with his dead child and his wife who was dying from consumption. Wesley arranged for the man's release and provided food and medical care for him. The man's wife died, but once freed from prison, the grateful man regained his health, started again in business, and eventually began a fund for the relief of other debtors.

John Wesley's only preoccupation with money was to whom should he give it. How is with us? In what measure has our heart become fixed on material goods? We don't have to be rich to be seekers of money. The world's way of looking at mammon is to pursue it. God's perspective is just the opposite: money is a tool for good, as we give it away. Money given to help others is money invested in heaven.

Like John Wesley, may we be known by God for our giving, rather than our seeking of money.

Riches have in all ages been the bane of genuine Christianity.

—from "The Mystery of Iniquity"

Suffering

The righteous cry out, and the Lord hears,
And delivers them out of all their troubles.
The Lord is near to those who have a broken heart,
And saves such as have a contrite spirit.
Many are the afflictions of the righteous,
But the Lord delivers him out of them all.

—Psalm 34:17–19

All suffering has a purpose. Ask Job. Ask John Wesley. Yes, he too had trials, sufferings, and persecutions. For all his many loyal supporters, he was passionately hated by thousands who wished to see him dead.

He also knew rejection on a more personal level. He had twice thought he would marry—and both women married other men. Yet he persevered. He received suffering as if God had handed it to him for a specific purpose. He knew that God measures out our trials in direct proportion to our needs. Yes, we *need* a measure of adversity in order for the Lord to show himself strong on our behalf and to invite us to draw closer to Him. Perseverance during suffering equals maturity.

The best helps to growth in grace are the . . . losses which befall us. We should receive them with all thankfulness, as preferable to all others, were it only on this account—that our will has no part therein.

The readiest way to escape from our sufferings is to be willing they should endure as long as God pleases. . . .

—from *A Plain Account of Christian Perfection*

What are your recent losses? Can you name each one and ask God to show you how each has actually been a gain in disguise? Maybe at least one of your trials isn't over yet. You may be in the process of loss now, and God's goal in sending it your way may still be impossible to see. But wait. God will make it clear.

John Wesley learned the secret of enduring trials: receive them with gratitude, not resentment. God will only measure out our sufferings in direct proportion to His goal.

Even in the greatest afflictions, we ought to testify to God that, in receiving them from His hand, we feel pleasure in the midst of the pain, from being afflicted by Him who loves us, and whom we love.

—from *A Plain Account of Christian Perfection*

Doctrine

For the time will come when they will not endure sound doctrine,
but according to their own desires, because they have itching ears,
they will heap up for themselves teachers; and they will turn their
ears away from the truth, and be turned aside to fables.

—2 Timothy 4:3–4

In his letter to William Dodd dated March 12, 1756, John Wesley cautions, "I try every Church and every doctrine by the Bible. This is the word by which we are to be judged in that day."

No doubt that part of Wesley's concern over doctrine was due to the grief he frequently got from others who accused him of teaching error. Everything that Wesley preached, therefore, had to pass a strict test in Wesley's mind as to its truth or error. It was a responsibility Wesley never took lightly. And when opposed, Wesley sought from his accusers, *scriptural* evidence for their charges.

Further, in his sermon, "On Corrupting the Word of God, Wesley identifies three ways false doctrine emerges:

1. Human ideas are added to Scripture.

2. Scripture is interpreted erroneously.

3. Scripture is softened by distorting the meaning in an effort not to offend.

Since John Wesley's day, we've seen hundreds of new doctrines from questionable leaders who have implemented one or all of the above methods of coming up with a new spin on the Bible. Those with itching ears eagerly follow such deviant doctrines to their own ruin.

Some groups have even been so bold as to offer additional "scriptures" with the claim that they're equal to the Bible. Such assertions would put Wesley in an immediate uproar. We too must reject those claims, standing with Wesley in the belief that all we need to know of eternal worth has already been given us. We need no new revelation. We need only to live out that which has already been revealed in God's Word.

Weigh everything by the Bible. What are we sure of but the Bible?

—from John Wesley's journal, June 14, 1774

15

On Sin

Therefore, if anyone is in Christ, he is a new creation; old things have passed away; behold, all things have become new.

—2 Corinthians 5:17

As Christians, we are new creations in Christ. But what exactly are the benefits of this new creation? John Wesley knew them well:

We allow that the state of a justified person is inexpressibly great and glorious. He is born again, "not of blood, nor of the flesh, nor of the will of man, but of God." He is a child of God, a member of Christ, an heir of the kingdom of heaven. "The peace of God, which passeth all understanding, keepeth his heart and mind in Christ Jesus." His very body is a "temple of the Holy Ghost," and an "habitation of God through the Spirit." He is "created anew in Christ Jesus:" He is *washed*, he is *sanctified*. His heart is purified by faith; he is cleansed "from the corruption that is in the world;" "the love of God is shed abroad in his heart by the Holy Ghost which is given unto him." And so long as he "walketh in love," (which he may always do,) he worships God in spirit and in truth. He keepeth the commandments of God, and doeth those things that are pleasing in his sight; so exercising himself as to "have a conscience void of offence, toward God and toward man:" And he has power both over outward and inward sin, even from the moment he is justified.

—from "On Sin in Believers"

Wesley was not shy in preaching the above good news—nor in living it. It was his heritage and it is *ours*. Today let's live in the full benefit of our new creation. Reread the above list, and insert your name in place of the pronoun *he*.

Enjoy your new life. It's already *yours*.

O Lord, take full possession of my heart, raise there your throne, and command there as you do in heaven. Being created by you, let me live for you; being created for you, let me always act for your glory; being redeemed by you, let me give to you what is yours; and let my spirit cling to you alone, for your name's sake.

—selected

The God Who Is There

"Am I a God near at hand," says the Lord,
"And not a God afar off? Can anyone hide himself in secret
places, so I shall not see him?" says the Lord;
"Do I not fill heaven and earth?" says the Lord.

—Jeremiah 23:23–24

[T]he omnipresence of God] is far too vast to be comprehended by the narrow limits of human understanding. The great God, the eternal, the almighty Spirit, is as unbounded in His presence as in His duration and power.

In condescension, indeed, to our weak understanding, He is said to dwell in heaven: but, strictly speaking, the heaven of heavens cannot contain Him; but He is in every part of His dominion. The universal God dwelleth in universal space.

—from "On the Omnipresence of God," Sermon 111

How can God be everywhere? How can He know my thoughts and at the same time know your thoughts? How can He hear (and answer) a billion prayers at once?

Wesley goes on to say in his sermon:

God acts everywhere, and, therefore, is everywhere; for it is an utter impossibility that any being, created or uncreated, should work where it is not. God acts in heaven, in earth, and under the earth, throughout the whole compass of His creation; by sustaining all things, without which everything would in an instant sink into its primitive nothing; by governing all, every moment superintending everything that He has made; strongly and sweetly influencing all, and yet without destroying the liberty of His rational creatures.

And what is the desired result of a God this infinite? Wesley says,

Spare no pains to preserve always a deep, a continual, a lively, and a joyful sense of His gracious presence . . . Cheerfully expect that He, before whom you stand, will ever guide you with His eye, will support you by His guardian hand, will keep you from all evil. . . .

Our omnipresent God guides us day by day, step by step. He is *here*.

In a word, there is no point of space, whether within or without the bounds of creation, where God is not.

— from "On the Omnipresence of God"

The Reading Christian

"Bring . . . the books, especially the parchments."
—2 Timothy 4:13

John Wesley was an avid reader—and writer. He urged pastors to spend their mornings (five hours!) reading books—and not necessarily the Bible. When some religious zealot boasted that he only read his Bible, Wesley responded with a charge of "rank enthusiasm."

In a letter to a fellow pastor, Wesley counseled, "What has exceedingly hurt you in time past . . . is want of reading. . . . By neglecting it, you have lost the taste for it."

The sole remedy for poor preaching, Wesley said, was "reading, with meditation and prayer." Any believer who would not read, could not be a "thorough Christian," Wesley continued.

What are your reading habits? Have you read the classics of the faith? How about great fiction that draws you closer to God?

Where to start? Here are several suggestions:

- *My Utmost For His Highest* by Oswald Chambers

- *Crime and Punishment* by Fyodor Dostoevsky

- *Les Miserable* by Victor Hugo

- *Way of Holiness* by Phoebe Palmer

- *The Christian's Secret of a Happy Life* by Hannah Whitall Smith

- *The Knowledge of the Holy* by A.W. Tozer

But if John Wesley himself were to suggest just one book every Christian should read, he might echo the advice he gave his Methodist society preachers more than two centuries ago: "Let every preacher read carefully over the life of David Brainerd."

David Brainerd (1718–1747) was a young American Christian who was devoted to prayer and to reaching the Native Americans. He lived only twenty-nine years, but his impact is still being felt today. Notable Christians from Wesley to William Carey to Henry Martyn to Jim Eliot have all been inspired by this classic work, which was put together from Brainerd's journals by Jonathan Edwards and published under the title, *The Life and Diary of the Reverend David Brainerd*. It has not been out of print since its publication more than two centuries ago.

And, yes, it's a must-read for every Christian.

Read the most useful books, and that regularly and constantly…

—from "Miscellaneous Counsels from John Wesley on Preaching"

18

Love of God

In this is love, not that we loved God, but that He loved us and
sent His Son to be the propitiation for our sins.

—1 John 4: 10

L oving God is not natural for us. Without instruction or apart from the intervention of the Holy Spirit, we would remain ignorant of God. Oh, we may hear of God in the same way we hear of a foreign leader or other newsworthy figure, but simply *hearing* does not translate to knowledge or love. John Wesley illustrates this in the following story:

> We read of an ancient king, who, being desirous to know what was the *natural language* of men, in order to bring the matter to a certain issue, made the following experiment: He ordered two infants, as soon as they were born, to be conveyed to a place prepared for them, where they were brought up without any instruction at all, and without ever hearing a human voice.
>
> And what was the result? When they were at length brought out of their confinement, they spoke no language at all; they uttered only inarticulate sounds, like those of other animals.
>
> Were two infants in like manner to be brought up from the womb without being instructed in any religion, there is little

room to doubt but (unless the grace of God interposed) the event would be just the same. They would have no religion at all: They would have no more knowledge of God than the beasts of the field, than the wild ass's colt. Such is natural religion, abstracted from traditional, and from the influences of God's Spirit!

—from "On Original Sin"

To know and love God is the result, not of something we do, but of something He does. God himself initiates a love relationship with His people. Throughout the Bible we see God coming to men and women, seeking fellowship, offering himself as the ultimate Friend, Redeemer, Father, Companion, Comforter, Defender.

He *first* loved us, 1 John 4:10 reminds us. Our only requirement is to *respond* to the love God has shown us and be wholly renewed.

By nature ye are . . . corrupted. By grace ye shall be wholly renewed.

—from "On Original Sin"

Using the Light of Scripture

*All Scripture is inspired by God and is useful to teach us what is true
and to make us realize what is wrong in our lives. It straightens us out
and teaches us to do what is right. It is God's way of preparing us in
every way, fully equipped for every good thing God wants us to do.*

—2 Timothy 3:16–17, NLT

The Word of God was absolutely central to the life and ministry
of John Wesley. He pored over the pages of the Bible with great
care, writing voluminously on what he saw there. Here's how he
advised Christians to read the Bible:

1. To set apart a little time, if you can, every morning and evening
   for that purpose

2. At each time if you have leisure, to read a chapter out of the
   Old, and one out of the New Testament: if you cannot do this,
   to take a single chapter, or a part of one

3. To read this with a single eye, to know the whole will of God, and
   a fixed resolution to do it. In order to know His will, you should,

4. Have a constant eye to the analogy of faith; the connection
   and harmony there is between those grand, fundamental doctrines, Original Sin, Justification by Faith, the New Birth,
   Inward and Outward Holiness.

5. Serious and earnest prayer should be constantly used, before we consult the oracles of God, seeing "scripture can only be understood thro' the same Spirit whereby it was given." Our reading should likewise be closed with prayer, that what we read may be written on our hearts.

6. It might also be of use, if while we read, we were frequently to pause, and examine ourselves by what we read, both with regard to our hearts, and lives. This would furnish us with matter of praise, where we found God had enabled us to conform to his blessed will, and matter of humiliation and prayer, where we were conscious of having fallen short.

God speaks to us through the Bible. He has much to say to encourage us. Plus, if we need guidance in a matter, it can come to us more effectively as our minds are renewed in the Word. Today, slowly read a favorite Psalm or chapter of the Bible, and do so with Wesley's instructions above in mind.

And whatever light you then receive, should be used to the uttermost, and that immediately. Let there be no delay. Whatever you resolve, begin to execute the first moment you can. So shall you find this word to be indeed the power of God unto present and eternal salvation.

—from John Wesley's preface to *Explanatory Notes upon the Old Testament*

20

Faithful Over a Few Things

His lord said to him, "Well done, good and faithful servant; you
were faithful over a few things, I will make you ruler over
many things. Enter into the joy of your lord."

—Matthew 25:21

These are the words every Christian longs to hear someday: *Well done, good and faithful servant.* What a joy it will be to hear our Heavenly Father utter those words to us.

But the condition for that to happen is determined *now.* We are not called to be John Wesley, nor Susanna or Charles or Samuel Wesley. They were faithful over what God gave *them.* We are never to compare ourselves with other Christians, says the apostle Paul in 2 Corinthians 10:12. We are simply to be faithful over the "few things" God has given us.

And know this: God measures out our few things in proportion to our strength. He never asks us to do what is not within our ability to do. Further, He gives us tasks that, when completed, bring us great joy, not resentment.

Our biggest concern should be this: that we do not become so preoccupied with our own "many things" that we have no time, nor the ability to discern the "few things" that God asks of us.

How do we know what we're to do? It's easy, really. First, we *ask* God. Then we watch, and when we see a need that we are able to meet with the gifts God has given us, we do so. The gifts God has given you are designed to match the needs of those around you. Don't let your preoccupation with this world obscure the work that prepares us for the next—and better—world.

O let your heart be whole with God! Seek your happiness in Him and Him alone. Beware that you cleave not to the dust! "This earth is not your place." See that you use this world as not abusing it; *use* the world, and *enjoy* God. Sit as loose to all things here below, as if you were a poor beggar. Be a good steward of the manifold gifts of God; that when you are called to give an account of your stewardship, He may say, "Well done, good and faithful servant, enter thou into the joy of thy Lord!"

—from "On Riches"

The Catholic Spirit

And when he was departed thence, he lighted on Jehonadab the son of
Rechab coming to meet him: and he saluted him, and said to him,
"Is thine heart right, as my heart is with thy heart?" And Jehonadab
answered, "It is." Jehu said, "If it be, give me thine hand."

—2 Kings 10:15, KJV

John Wesley was an ardent foe of religious bigotry. He acknowledged that there are significant differences between Christians, but they must not be weapons of division. The unity of the faith was more important to Wesley than the elevation of one person's opinion over another's. It was that thinking that caused him to write his now-famous sermon, "The Catholic Spirit." In that sermon, Wesley notes,

> A [Christian] of a catholic spirit is one who, in the above-mentioned [verse], gives his hand to all whose hearts are right with his heart. [He is] one who knows how to value, and praise God for all the advantages he enjoys with regard to the knowledge of the things of God.
>
> He is the man of a truly catholic spirit, who bears all these continually upon his heart; who having an unspeakable tenderness for their persons, and longing for their welfare, does not cease to commend them to God in prayer, as well as to plead their cause before men; who speaks comfortably to

them, and labours, by all his words, to strengthen their hands in God. He assists them to the uttermost of his power in all things, spiritual and temporal. He is ready "to spend and be spent for them;" yea, to lay down his life for their sake.

—from "The Catholic Spirit"

Are you of one heart with other Christians everywhere? Can you find more in common with those who love the Lord than you find differences? The true Christians of a "Catholic spirit" are not divided.

Keep you your opinion; I mine; and that as steadily as ever. You need not even endeavour to come over to me, or bring me over to you. I do not desire you to dispute those points, or to hear or speak one word concerning them.

Let all opinions alone on one side and the other: only "give me thine hand."

—from "The Catholic Spirit"

22

Pardoning Love

In this is love, not that we loved God, but that He loved us and
sent His Son to be the propitiation for our sins.

—1 John 4:10

How came you . . . to love Him at first?

Was it not because you knew that He loved you? Did you, could you, love God at all, till you tasted and saw that He was gracious; that He was merciful to you a sinner?

What avails then controversy, or strife of words? Out of thy own mouth! You own you had no love to God till you were sensible of His love to you. And whatever expressions any sinner who loves God uses, to denote God's love to Him, you will always upon examination find, that they directly or indirectly imply forgiveness. . . .

He who was offended is now reconciled. . . . A confidence then in a pardoning God is essential to saving faith. The forgiveness of sins is one of the first of those unseen things whereof faith is the evidence.

—from "An Earnest Appeal to Men of Reason and Religion"

So often we measure our faith by how much we love God—or *think* we love God. And yet Christianity is more about God's love for us than our love for Him. *He* first loved us. Our love for Him, then, is a proper response to His initiating love.

How did God demonstrate the depth of His love for us? He *gave* that which was dearest to Him—His Son. We find it hard to imagine God having the ability to sacrifice something for any reason. After all, He is God. What sort of sacrifice can God make? And yet, that's exactly the point. The God of the universe so loved us as to sacrifice the unthinkable—His most prized object of His love: His Son.

To grasp this sort of love that *must* be accomplished in order to secure our pardon from sin is to be transformed. We cannot look at the love of God as a mere abstraction when we understand that it *cost* God dearly. We can then understand why we too are to love everyone—even our enemies.

Pardoning love is still the root of all.

—from "An Earnest Appeal to Men of Reason and Religion"

23

The Eyes of Faith

Now faith is the substance of things hoped for,
the evidence of things not seen.

—Hebrews 11:1

F aith is that divine evidence whereby the spiritual man discerneth God, and the things of God. [Faith] is to the spiritual world what sense is to the natural. It is the spiritual sensation of every soul that is born of God.

— from "An Earnest Appeal to Men of Reason and Religion"

For the Christian, it is through the eyes of faith that we see things hoped for—things not seen by the physical eye.

At our new birth, we are given this new sense by which to perceive the realities of God. And day by day, it's by use of this organ of faith that we move along our journey, step by uncertain step.

The eye of faith kept Wesley through many trials. Persecution, the betrayal of friends, temptations, bodily discomfort, even marriage to whom he described as an impossible woman—all were triumphed over through the eye of faith.

Many days John Wesley awoke unaware of what new trials awaited him. But by faith, he *knew* God had set aside the day with all of its joys or sorrows.

Likewise today, you don't know what God has planned. But you have the same God as John Wesley. Use your eye of faith to move ahead today. Look at every event knowing that God has already been there. Know that other believers have also been there. Nothing you encounter is new under the sun. Someone somewhere is going through the same trials you are. They, like you, will only come through by faith.

Learn to see today's problems as measured out by God in deliberation that you might strengthen your spiritual eyesight.

Faith, according to the scriptural account, is the eye of the newborn soul.

—from "An Earnest Appeal to Men of Reason and Religion"

24

Stewardship

*Give an account of your stewardship, for you
can no longer be steward.*

—Luke 16:2

G od has entrusted us with our soul—an immortal spirit, made in the image of God; together with all the powers and faculties thereof: understanding, imagination, memory, will, and a train of affections, either included in it or closely dependent upon it. [Also] love and hatred, joy and sorrow, respecting present good and evil; desire and aversion, hope and fear, respecting that which is to come . . . Now, of all these, it is certain, we are only stewards.

God has entrusted us with these powers and faculties, not that we may employ them according to our own will, but according to the express orders which He has given us—although it is true that, in doing His will, we most effectually secure our own happiness; seeing it is herein only that we can be happy, either in time or in eternity. Thus we are to use our understanding, our imagination, our memory, wholly to the glory of Him that gave them.

—from "The Good Steward"

The key to happiness is found in the right stewardship of all God's gifts to us. It's through employing the gifts of God in fulfilling the will of God, that we reap true happiness as a benefit. To the contrary, to pursue our own plans of happiness—to *spend* rather to *invest* the gifts God has given us—can only result in emptiness and shallow living.

Where are we today in the stewardship of our soul? Is it—along with all its faculties—truly His, or have we held back the best for ourselves?

Think of some of the gifts God has uniquely given you. Name them out loud.

Think also of the gifts common to all of us: the gift of thought, the gift of creativity, the gift of memory, the gift of dreaming for the future, the gift of humor, the gift of observation. So many gifts we take for granted!

Our soul is the very essence of who we are and must be daily tended to as a garden. We must be faithful stewards of His gifts if we would like to be happy.

Now, reader, what is your character, and what has been your conduct? God will soon call you to give an account of your stewardship. Have you been faithful to God, faithful to your own soul, and the souls of others?

—from "Stewardship"

25

Dependence

And when you pray, you shall not be like the hypocrites. For they love to pray standing in the synagogues and on the corners of the streets, that they may be seen by men. Assuredly, I say to you, they have their reward. But you, when you pray, go into your room, and when you have shut your door, pray to your Father who is in the secret place; and your Father who sees in secret will reward you openly. And when you pray, do not use vain repetitions as the heathen do. For they think that they will be heard for their many words. Therefore do not be like them. For your Father knows the things you have need of before you ask Him.

—Matthew 6:5–9

We all have needs. You certainly know some of your needs. And so does God. And every need is fitted perfectly to the provision of God for you.

Your Father knoweth what things ye have need of. We do not pray to inform God of our wants. Omniscient as He is, He cannot be informed of any thing which He knew not before: and He is always willing to relieve them.

The chief thing wanting is, a fit disposition on our part to receive His grace and blessing. Consequently, one great office of prayer is, to produce such a disposition in us: to exercise our dependence on God; to increase our desire of the things we ask for; to us so sensible of our wants, that we may never cease wrestling till we have prevailed for the blessing.

—from *Explanatory Notes on the New Testament,* Matthew 6

God does not need us to pray to inform Him of our wants; He already knows before we ask. But for our sakes, He invites us to pray in order to increase our dependence on Him, to increase our awareness of Him as our provider, and to strengthen our faith. When we pray earnestly and see God answer, it builds trust in us. And the goal of prayer is always two-fold: to bring glory to God and to cement our dependence on Him.

Let prayer do its work on you. Let it make you more open to receiving from your generous Heavenly Father.

Watch, that ye may pray; and pray, that ye may watch.

—from *Explanatory Notes on the New Testament,* 1 Peter

26

The Remedy
for Prayerlessness

Then He came to the disciples and found them sleeping, and said to Peter, "What! Could you not watch with Me one hour? Watch and pray, lest you enter into temptation. The spirit indeed is willing, but the flesh is weak."

—Matthew 26:40–41

Hindered in prayer? Does your mind wander? Eyes get heavy? Then you're in good company. Many Christians seem to want improvement in their prayer life. So why does prayer sometimes seem so hard?

Wesley cited two obstacles: first, our own human nature that is disinclined to the practice of prayer, save the few bullet prayers we may send upward during a frantic day, and second, our enemy, who certainly seeks to keep us from praying. But if we will recognize these hindrances, we can overcome them.

> Nature and the devil will always oppose private prayer—but it is worthwhile to break through. That it is a cross will not hinder its being a blessing—nay, often the more reluctance the greater blessing.
>
> —from a letter to Dorothy Furly, September 25, 1757

Need more joy? Pray through.

Need deliverance from temptation. Prayer will deliver you.

Need a blessing? It's hiding behind that unprayed prayer.

The more forceful the opposition, the more we *must* pray. There is a great blessing hiding behind every unprayed prayer.

God does nothing but in answer to prayer.

—from *A Plain Account of Christian Perfection*

27

Righteousness, Sanctification, and Redemption

But of Him you are in Christ Jesus, who became for us wisdom from
God—and righteousness and sanctification and redemption—that,
as it is written, "He who glories, let him glory in the Lord."

—1 Corinthians 1:30–31

Christian faith is . . . not only an assent to the whole gospel of Christ, but also a full reliance on the blood of Christ; a trust in the merits of His life, death, and resurrection; a [dependency] upon Him as our atonement and our life, as given for us, and living in us; and, in consequence hereof, a closing with Him, and cleaving to Him, as our "wisdom, righteousness, sanctification, and redemption," or, in one word, our salvation.

—from "Salvation by Faith"

To unbelievers, Jesus Christ is a historical figure of some interest—but not the Son of God. And His death was certainly, not to them, an atonement for the sins of mankind. They maintain there was no resurrection after His death. The gospel is thus a mystery to unbelievers—no more than a history lesson.

But for the Christian, the reality of who Christ is plumbs depths we can never fully fathom in this life. In that way, the gospel is a mystery to us too. A glorious mystery. How is it that we, the believers in Christ, can be so dependent on Christ as our life? How can this God whom no one can see, become to us our wisdom, our righteousness, our sanctification, and our redemption?

How can that which is so hidden from unbelievers be so very precious to us who believe?

The gracious scheme of salvation by faith, which depends on his own sovereign will alone . . . was but darkly discovered under the law; is now totally hid from unbelievers; and has heights and depths which surpass all the knowledge even of true believers.

—from *Explanatory Notes on the Bible,* Ephesians 1

28

The Medicine of Life

Then they will deliver you up to tribulation and kill you, and you will be hated by all nations for My name's sake. And then many will be offended, will betray one another, and will hate one another. Then many false prophets will rise up and deceive many. And because lawlessness will abound, the love of many will grow cold.

—Matthew 24:9–12

Among the several signs of His return, Jesus says that the love of many will grow cold, due to lawlessness. Wherever there is a departure from doing things God's way, or lawlessness, there is an ebbing of love. Without God, men become lovers of themselves, looking out for their self-interests, rather than the interests of others.

John Wesley placed a premium on love, the badge of a Christian. Not merely speaking about love, but a love that seeks out ways to do good for others—particularly to those who are trapped in what Wesley calls "a lifeless formal religion," or to those who have no knowledge of God at all. Our love for such people, says Wesley, acts as a medicine of life.

For example, Wesley and a fellow preacher were dinner guests at the home of a well-to-do man who had a daughter noted for her rare beauty. The young woman had been impressed by Wesley's preaching, but had not surrendered her heart. At one point, Wesley's insensitive colleague took the young woman's hand and called attention to the ornate rings she was wearing. "What do you think of this, sir, for a

Methodist hand," Wesley's friend said. The embarrassed young woman, realizing Wesley's noted aversion to costly jewelry, turned crimson. Wesley was likewise embarrassed, but with a kindly smile, he simply said, "The hand is very beautiful."

Wesley's gracious remark removed the sting of the remark and later that evening, the young woman attended Wesley's preaching—without her jewels—and soon became a strong Christian.

It was the picture of graciousness toward others. The love of God in action.

This religion we long to see established in the world: a religion of love and joy and peace, having its seat in the inmost soul, but ever showing itself by its fruits, continually springing forth not only in all innocence—for love worketh no ill to his neighbor—but likewise in every kind of beneficence, spreading virtue and happiness all around it.

—from "An Earnest Appeal to Men of Reason and Religion"

It's up to us to be a dispenser to others of the medicine of life. Every day brings at least one such opportunity. Watch for divine appointments in which you're called upon to be the salve for someone's hurt or to speak with kindness and grace.

29

Altogether a Christian

For "who has known the mind of the Lord that he may instruct Him?"
But we have the mind of Christ.

—1 Corinthians 2:16

Paul urged believers to have the mind of Christ:

Let this mind be in you which was also in Christ Jesus, who, being in the form of God, did not consider it robbery to be equal with God, but made Himself of no reputation, taking the form of a bondservant, and coming in the likeness of men. And being found in appearance as a man, He humbled Himself and became obedient to the point of death, even the death of the cross" (Phil. 2:5–8).

The mind is the factory from which come all our thoughts—both good and bad. Those thoughts take root and eventually burst into action—both good and bad.

For the mind without Christ, there can be no access to the kinds of thoughts that make for a holy and truly *good* life. But we who believe are blessed to have the mind of Christ offered to us: a mind that produces only thoughts of peace, soundness, meekness, and mercy, but never destructive thoughts or suggestions of evil to another.

Jesus demonstrated what the mind of Christ looks like when He suffered His enemies to nail Him to the cross for their (and our) sins. To have the mind of Christ is to have a mind motivated by true humility and concern for others, rather than primarily self—to take on the humility that Jesus assumed when He became a servant in the likeness of man.

The natural mind cannot fathom this selfless mind of Christ, this severity of holiness that is expressed as pure love. But that's what we're called to live out daily.

Go on, in full pursuit of all the mind that was in Christ, of inward and then outward holiness; so shall you be not almost but altogether a Christian. So shall your finish your course with joy.

—from "On Redeeming the Time"

30

Creativity

For since the creation of the world His invisible attributes are
clearly seen, being understood by the things that are made,
even His eternal power and Godhead. . . .

—Romans 1:20

Each of us is given some measure of ability in which to creatively express something about the truth of life—and of God. The doorway to our creativity is our imagination. Not our natural imagination, but our renewed imagination, our surrendered imagination. We can easily see the results of the fallen imagination in much of modern expression. And we can see the fruit of the Christ-filled imagination in works by artists who knowingly used their gifts for God's glory. Michelangelo is one obvious example. "I live and love in God's peculiar light," he declared, regarding his art, which almost universally was an expression of his faith.

But was John Wesley an artist? Yes!

If his massive collections of sermons, commentaries, and medical books aren't enough, there is also his important work of translating German and Latin hymns into English. He also composed hymns and wrote poetry.

But God's artists aren't all poets, painters, musicians, and the like. God gifts certain of His people with other arts. many of these gifts are seemingly ordinary but highly practical: the art of cooking, inventing,

building, running a business, teaching others and, perhaps the art most closely originating with God, the art of loving.

No matter what our talents, Christians should be the most creative people on earth. We should be serious about the gifts God has given us—especially since they are a human reflection of His divinity.

Daily surrender your abilities to God. Allow Him to give you the ideas, the strength, and the vision to complete your creative mission on earth.

If you ever need to be reminded as to God's wonderful ability to create, just look in a mirror. He created you and me in His image. Behind that reflection in the mirror is a body full of God's highest creation. Individually, we are an expression of His creativity. We have each been given "talents" in the form of gifts that glorify God. Use yours.

You have one talent now: If you expect five more, so much the rather improve that you have. And the more you expect to receive hereafter, the more labor for God now.

—from "Satan's Devices"

31

Private Devotions

You are my God, and I will praise You;
You are my God, I will exalt You.
Oh, give thanks to the Lord, for He is good!
For His mercy endures forever.

—Psalm 118:28–29

One of Wesley's admonitions to believers was to set aside a daily time of private devotion. But what to pray? Should we recite the same staid prayers we learned as a child? No! Prayer must be from the heart. We must "cry out" Wesley says.

The generality of Christians, as soon as they rise, are accustomed to use some kind of prayer; and probably to use the same form still which they learned when they were eight or ten years old.

Now I do not condemn those who proceed thus (though many do) as mocking God; though they have used the same form, without any variation, for twenty or thirty years together. But surely there is "a more excellent way" of ordering our private devotions.

Consider both your outward and inward state, and vary your prayers accordingly.

For instance: Suppose your outward state is prosperous; suppose you are in a state of health, ease, and plenty, having your lot cast among kind relations, good neighbours, and agreeable friends, that love you and you them; then your outward state manifestly calls for praise and thanksgiving to God.

On the other hand, if you are in a state of adversity; if God has laid trouble upon your loins; if you are in poverty, in distress; if you are in any imminent danger; if you are in pain and sickness; then you are clearly called to pour out your soul before God in such prayer as is suited to your circumstances.

Is your soul in heaviness, either from a sense of sin, or through manifold temptations? Then let your prayer consist of such confessions, petitions, and supplications, as are agreeable to your distressed situation of mind.

On the contrary, is your soul in peace? Are you rejoicing in God? Then say, with the Psalmist: "Thou art my God, and I will love thee: Thou art my God, and I will praise thee." You may, likewise, when you have time, add to your other devotions a little reading and meditation, and perhaps a psalm of praise,—the natural effusion of a thankful heart. . . .

You must certainly see that this is "a more excellent way" than the poor dry form which you used before.

—from "The More Excellent Way"

Whatever your circumstances or mood today, you can pray accordingly. Don't hold back. Pour out your heart! Pray over your every pressing need. Take time to pray clear through. If all is going well for you, give thanks. Then pray for others who are going through a rough patch.

32

Childlike Trust

*Assuredly, I say to you, whoever does not receive the kingdom
of God as a little child will by no means enter it.*

—Mark 10:15

S omeone has disappointed us. Perhaps we even imagine God has not
come through for us. We become skeptical, untrusting. We are on the
lookout for the motives of others. Perhaps we're even aware of our own
questionable motives when dealing with others. It can happen slowly,
over a period of time, but we become hardened; we become *adults*.

But the kingdom of God is open only to those who will receive it
as children. Yes, God calls us to be childlike. Not *childish,* but childlike: pure, trusting, *un*-cynical.

Sure, this can cause us to be thought naïve by others. And perhaps
we will miss seeing someone's wrong motives towards us. But that's
their sin, not ours.

Charles Wesley deeply loved his brother, John. The two were as
solid of brothers as you'd want to find. And yet they were so different
in one respect. Charles said of John's childlikeness trust, "My brother
was born for the benefit of knaves." But John countered, "My brother
suspects everybody; I suspect nobody . . . and he is more frequently
duped than I."

What irony: the one who is most trusting being the *least* taken advantage of, and the skeptical one frequently the target of deceit.

It's not a sin to be as innocent as a child. It's a blessing. May God help us to live this blessing of childlikeness. May we truly trust our Heavenly Father as His little children.

A man cannot have a childlike confidence in God till he knows he is a child of God.

—from "The Scripture Way of Salvation"

33

Confession

Confess your sins to each other and pray for each other so that
you may be healed. The earnest prayer of a righteous person
has great power and wonderful results.

—James 5:16, NLT

Unless you are a Roman Catholic, the practice of verbally confessing sins to another person may seem strange—perhaps even embarrassing. But it's cleansing. Wesley recognized the benefit of having at least one other person with whom to share this ancient practice. Here are the guidelines Wesley used when he met with others to examine the "true state of his soul."

In order to "confess our faults one to another," and pray one for another that we may be healed, we intend:

1. To meet once a week, at the least.

2. To come punctually at the hour appointed.

3. To begin with singing or prayer.

4. To speak each of us in order, freely and plainly, the true state of our soul, with the faults we have committed in

thought, word, or deed, and the temptations we have felt since our last meeting.

5. To desire some person among us (thence called a Leader) to speak his own state first, and then to ask the rest, in order, as many and as searching questions as may be, concerning their state, sins, and temptations.

A word of caution not mentioned by Wesley: be careful to whom you open your heart. The desired closer union mentioned below must not be entered into with those who are not likely to keep a confidence or who are not spiritually mature.

But are there real advantages in sharing with others? Wesley thought so:

Great and many are the advantages which have ever since flowed from this closer union of the believers with each other. They prayed for one another, that they might be healed of the faults they had confessed; and it was so.

The chains were broken, the bands were burst in sunder, and sin had no more dominion over them. Many were delivered from the temptations out of which, till then, they found no way to escape. They were built up in our most holy faith. They rejoiced in the Lord more abundantly. They were strengthened in love, and more effectually provoked to abound in every good work.

—from "A Plain Account of the People Called Methodists"

34

Small Sins

And of His fullness we have all received, and grace for grace.

—John 1:16

As very little dust will disorder a clock, and the smallest bit of sand will obscure our sight, so the least grain of sin upon the heart will hinder its right motion toward God.

—from *A Plain Account of Christian Perfection*

Sin short-circuits our life. Even small sins are dangerous because we tend to pay them no mind. After all, if we've conquered our large sins, we tend to make allowances for smaller sins, like gossip, anger, envy, covetousness, or allowing our thoughts to linger a bit longer on that lovely creature at the desk next to ours.

But *all* sin destroys. The clock will be broken in time by the mites of dust, as well as by the blows of a club.

Which little sins do you treat lightly? Put an end to them. You can live without them.

Perhaps you will say, "This is only a little thing: it is a mere trifle." I answer, If it be, you are the more inexcusable before God and man. What! will you disobey a plain commandment of God for *a mere trifle?* God forbid! Is it a trifle to sin against God,—to set his authority at nought? Is this a little thing? Nay, remember, there can be no little sin, till we can find a little God!

—from "On Obedience to Pastors"

35

Sins of Omission

If we confess our sins, He is faithful and just to forgive us our
sins and to cleanse us from all unrighteousness.

—1 John 1:9

God has mercy on all our sins—those of commission and those of omission. But often we're more likely to see our sins of commission—the words spoken in anger, the sudden lustful impulse, the doubts and fears—than our sins of omission. What sins are we most likely to omit? Here are a few common ones:

We're sometimes forgetful of our ministry to our own family members. We forget to praise the child who has done well, call the lonely aging parent, and tell our mate how much we love them.

There are needs in our communities that we easily neglect. Opportunities abound to visit nursing homes, volunteer at a local school, and get involved in local civic groups that impact our town.

Perhaps we have money we should be investing in God's kingdom by supporting excellent ministries.

Is there a job at church with our name on it?

And perhaps most important of all, are we omitting time with God? Do we sin by not taking time to know Him better?

In each of these cases, not only do we fail to be fully Christian in practice, but we also forfeit the benefits that accompany *doing* something good. Take just a moment and ask yourself if God has been nudging you about any sins of omission.

Till the sin, whether of omission or commission, be removed, all comfort is false and deceitful. It is only skinning the wound over, which still festers and rankles beneath. Look for no peace within, till you are at peace with God; which cannot be without "fruits meet for repentance."

—from "The Wilderness State"

36

Full Possession

For you were bought at a price; therefore glorify God in your
body and in your spirit, which are God's.

—1 Corinthians 6:20

There is a secret to being used of God. John Wesley knew that secret. Others have known it too. The secret is simply total abandonment to God. Nothing may be held in reserve. There must be no rivals for our affections. God requires *all*.

> When He has taken the full possession of our heart; when He reigns therein without a rival, the Lord of every motion there; when we dwell in Christ, and Christ in us, we are one with Christ, and Christ with us; then we are completely happy; then we live "all the life that is hid with Christ in God;" then, and not till then, we properly experience what that word meaneth, "God is love; and whosoever dwelleth in love, dwelleth in God, and God in Him."
>
> —from "Spiritual Worship"

Happiness is being one with Christ, and Christ being one with us—a life hidden with Christ in God. This is the God-owned life.

God will not refuse the fully surrendered soul.

O that we may heartily surrender our wills to thine, and that we may unchangeably cleave unto it, with the greatest and most entire affection to all thy commands.

O that there may abide for ever in us, such a strong and powerful sense of thy mighty love towards us in CHRIST JESUS, as may constrain us freely and willingly to please thee, in the constant exercise of righteousness and mercy, temperance and charity, meekness and patience, truth and fidelity; together with such an humble, con-tented, and peaceable spirit, as may adorn the religion of our LORD and Master.

Yea, let it ever be the joy of our hearts to be righteous as you art righteous; to be merciful as You, our heavenly Father, art merciful; to be holy, as you who has called us art holy, in all manner of conversation; to be endued with thy divine wisdom; and to resemble thee in faithfulness and truth.

O that the example of our blessed Savior may be always dear unto us, that we may cheerfully follow him in every holy temper, and in delight to do thy will, O God Let these desires, which you have given us, never die or languish in our hearts, but be kept always alive, always in vigor and force, by the perpetual inspirations of the Holy Ghost.

—from "Prayers for Families"

37

On Conscience

I myself always strive to have a conscience without
offense toward God and men.

—Acts 24:16

To John Wesley, the Holy Spirit was essential in the searching of one's conscience. Further, a Christian conscience must be the daily rule of living, and nothing must be admitted to our lives and no deed committed by us that violates this Spirit-searched conscience.

What is conscience, in the Christian sense? It is that faculty of the soul which, by the assistance of the grace of God, sees at one and the same time:

1. Our own tempers and lives,—the real nature and quality of our thoughts, words, and actions;

2. The rule whereby we are to be directed; and,

3. The agreement or disagreement therewith.

Conscience implies, First, the faculty a man has of knowing himself; of discerning, both in general and in particular, his own tempers, thoughts, words, and actions. But this is not possible for him to do, without the assistance of the Spirit of God. Otherwise, self-love, and, indeed, every other irregular passion, would disguise and wholly conceal him from himself.

Secondly, a knowledge of the rule whereby he is to be directed in every particular; which is the word of God.

Thirdly, a knowledge that all his thoughts, and words, and actions are conformable to that rule. In all the offices of conscience, the "unction of the Holy One" is indispensably needful. Without this, neither could we clearly discern our lives or tempers; nor could we judge of the rule whereby we are to walk, or of our conformity of disconformity to it.

—from "On Conscience"

The challenge today is to not allow our conscience to be dulled by the world's standards of behavior, nor by our own unregulated passions, nor by that most base of all motives: self love. Follow your *true* conscience. Follow the dictates of the Holy Spirit as He searches your heart.

Therefore, if you desire to have your conscience always quick to discern, and faithful to accuse or excuse you, if you would preserve it always sensible and tender, be sure to obey it at all events; continually listen to its admonitions, and steadily follow them. Whatever it directs you to do, according to the word of God, do; however grievous to flesh and blood. Whatever it forbids, if the prohibition be grounded on the word of God, see you do it not; however pleasing it may be to flesh and blood.

—from "On Conscience"

38

Seeking
Spiritual Gifts

But earnestly desire the best gifts. And yet I show
you a more excellent way.

—1 Corinthians 12:31

Many Christians desire spiritual gifts. Sometimes they long for the miraculous gifts found in the New Testament church. But Wesley cautions that those gifts diminished for one reason: because love, the most important of the gifts of the Spirit, had likewise vanished. The Christians were living like the heathen and holding to a dead form of religion.

Spiritual gifts are wonderful. Paul says we are to seek them. But he also says there is something even more excellent than spiritual gifts: love.

It does not appear that these extraordinary gifts of the Holy Ghost were common in the church for more than two or three centuries We seldom hear of them after that fatal period when the Emperor Constantine called himself a Christian, and from a vain imagination of promoting the Christian cause thereby heaped riches, and power, and honour, upon the Christians in general; but in particular upon the Christian clergy. From this time they almost totally ceased; very few instances of the kind were found. The cause of this was not (as has been vulgarly supposed) "because there was no more occasion for them," because all the world was become Christian. This is a miserable mistake; not a twentieth part of it was then nominally Christian.

The real cause was, "the love of many," almost of all Christians, so called, was "waxed cold." The Christians had no more of the Spirit of Christ than the other Heathens. The Son of Man, when He came to examine His Church, could hardly "find faith upon earth." This was the real cause why the extraordinary gifts of the Holy Ghost were no longer to be found in the Christian Church—because the Christians were turned Heathens again, and had only a dead form left.

—from "The More Excellent Way"

Has God blessed you with a spiritual gift? If so, use it in love, or risk losing it. If you say you have no gift, then seek a gift, but first learn the "more excellent way."

Faith, hope, love—Are the sum of perfection on earth; love alone is the sum of perfection in heaven.

—from *Explanatory Notes on the New Testament,* 1 Corinthians 13

39

Humor

A merry heart does good, like medicine.
—Proverbs 17:22

In today's language, John Wesley was what we'd call "focused." He knew his calling and gave his full life to it. He didn't have time for a regular family life nor for the amusements and recreations common to many of his peers. Early in his career he remarked, "leisure and I have taken leave of each other."

But fortunately, Wesley's humor did not also take leave of him. It did show itself on occasion—and usually in a very witty way. One day Wesley's path crossed with an oaf who refused to grant Wesley the right of way. Looking at Wesley with contempt, the man sneered, "I never give way for a fool." Without a thought, Wesley simply replied, "I always do," and stepped out of the man's way, allowing him to pass by first.

Another instance of humor was at the expense of his traveling companion, Michael Fenwick, who was disappointed that Wesley had never mentioned his name in his published magazine. Upon hearing this, Wesley made amends in the next edition by noting "I left Epworth and at about one o'clock preached at Clayworth. I think no one was unmoved by my message but Michael Fenwick, who fell fast asleep under an adjoining hayrick."

On a walk near Billingsgate Market, Wesley and his companion encountered two fishwives quarreling furiously, overflowing with angry emotion toward each other. Wesley's companion said, "Pray sir, let us go on. I cannot stand this." But Wesley, taken with the force and earnestness of the women, said, "Stay, my friend, and learn how to preach!"

Humor is good. Laughter is medicine, the book of Proverbs teaches. A Christian heart is a joyful heart. Look for the humor God has given your life.

Don't be reluctant to be a happy Christian.

A sour godliness is the devil's religion.

—quoted in *The Methodist Book Concern*, 1903

40

Repentance

God overlooked people's former ignorance about these things,
but now he commands everyone everywhere to turn
away from idols and turn to him.

—Acts 17:30, NLT

R epentance frequently means an inward change, a change of mind from sin to holiness. But we now speak of it in quite a different sense, as it is one kind of self-knowledge, the knowledge of knowing ourselves sinners, yea, guilty, helpless sinners, even though we know we are children of God.

—from "The Repentance of Believers"

If we're not mindful, we can forget from whence we came—and what we are without Christ. We were born into sin. We were simply lost sheep without a shepherd. And then we met Christ. We repented of our sins and turned toward holiness. But as Wesley points out, there is another repentance appropriate for those who believe. Wesley describes this repentance as a knowledge of ourselves and of our sinfulness apart from Christ. If we ever lose this self-knowledge, we can tend toward self-righteousness. Not only did we need a Savior before we knew Christ, but we still need a Savior as we continue in the faith.

Christ was your Savior yesterday. He will again be your Savior tomorrow. But best of all, He is your Savior *today*.

Believe the glad tidings of great salvation, which God hath prepared for all people. Believe that He who is "the brightness of His Father's glory, the express image of his person," is "able to save unto the uttermost all that come unto God through Him."

He is able to save you from all the sin that still remains in your heart.

He is able to save you from all the sin that cleaves to all your words and actions.

He is able to save you from sins of omission, and to supply whatever is wanting in you.

It is true, this is impossible with man; but with God-Man all things are possible.

—from "The Repentance of Believers"

41

The Lord's Supper

For as often as you eat this bread and drink this cup,
you proclaim the Lord's death till He comes.

—1 Corinthians 11:26

John Wesley put high importance on the celebration of the Lord's Supper. It wasn't a meaningless ritual; it had power in the life of the Christian. In 1787 he wrote the tract "The Duty of Constant Communion."

The First reason why it is the duty of every Christian so to do is, because it is a plain command of Christ. . . . Observe, too, that this command was given by our Lord when He was just laying down His life for our sakes. They are, therefore, as it were, His dying words to all his followers.

A Second reason is, because the benefits of doing it are so great to all that do it in obedience to Him: the forgiveness of our past sins and the present strengthening and refreshing of our souls.

In this world we are never free from temptations. Whatever way of life we are in, whatever our condition be, whether we are sick or well, in trouble or at ease, the enemies of our souls are watching to lead us into sin. And too often they prevail over us. Now, when we are convinced of having sinned against God, what surer way have we of procuring pardon from Him, than the "showing forth the Lord's death;" and beseeching Him, for the sake of His Son's sufferings, to blot out all our sins?

. . . Let every one, therefore, who has either any desire to please God, or any love of his own soul, obey God, and consult the good of his own soul, by communicating every time he can; like the first Christians, with whom the Christian sacrifice was a constant part of the Lord's day service. And for several centuries they received it almost every day . . . Accordingly, those that joined in the prayers of the faithful never failed to partake of the blessed sacrament. What opinion they had of any who turned his back upon it, we may learn from that ancient canon: "If any believer join in the prayers of the faithful, and go away without receiving the Lord's Supper, let him be excommunicated, as bringing confusion into the church of God." It is the duty of every Christian to receive the Lord's Supper as often as he can.

—from "The Duty of Constant Communion"

How precious is the celebration of the Lord's Supper to Christians! We receive strength, renewal and blessing from sharing the loaf and the cup with our brothers and sisters. And remember, it was through "taking and eating" that Adam and Eve lost paradise. And it was Christ who crushed Satan, with the breaking of His own body and the spilling of His blood, and biding us, "take, eat."

If today is not a day in which you can celebrate the Lord in this way, take time to reflect on this glorious provision by our Lord. And the next opportunity you have to do so, receive with joy the blood and the body of the Lord Jesus, realizing its full import.

42

Treasures
in Heaven

*Do not lay up for yourselves treasures on earth, where moth and rust destroy
and where thieves break in and steal; but lay up for yourselves treasures in
heaven, where neither moth nor rust destroys and where thieves do not break
in and steal. For where your treasure is, there your heart will be also.*

—Matthew 6:19–21

O ye lovers of money, hear the word of the Lord! Suppose
ye that money, though multiplied as the sand of the
sea, can give happiness? Then you are "given up to a strong
delusion, to believe a lie;"—a palpable lie, confuted daily by
a thousand experiments.

Open your eyes!

Look all around you! Are the richest men the happiest?
Have those the largest share of content who have the largest
possessions? Is not the very reverse true? Is it not a
common observation, that the richest of men are, in general,
the most discontented, the most miserable? Had not the far
greater part of them more content when they had less
money?

Look into your breasts. If you are increased in goods, are
you proportionably increased in happiness? You have more
substance; but have you more content? You know that in
seeking happiness from riches, you are only striving to drink

out of empty cups. And let them be painted and gilded ever so finely, they are empty still.

—from "The Danger of Riches"

Don't imagine that John Wesley was against money itself. His counsel was against *riches,* not money. Christians, Wesley maintained, should learn the "right use" of money. By this, he taught:

1. Christians should "gain all [they] can through honest industry."

2. Foolishness expenditures are not to be indulged in, but rather, Christians should endeavor to "save all [they] can."

3. The third and final rule Wesley taught was that Christians must "give all [they] can." Specifically, Christians must first use their hard-earned money to provide for their family's needs, and "If when this is done there be an overplus left, then do good to them that are of the household of faith."

You will have no reward in heaven for what you lay up: you will for what you lay out. Every pound you put into the earthly bank is sunk: it brings no interest above. But every pound you give to the poor is put into the bank of heaven. And it will bring glorious interest; yea, and such as will be accumulating to all eternity.

—from "The More Excellent Way"

43

A Present Possession

For by grace ye are saved through faith.

—Ephesians 2:8, KJV

[Our salvation] is a present salvation. It is something attainable, yea, actually attained, on earth, by those who are partakers of this faith. For thus saith the Apostle to the believers at Ephesus, and in them to the believers of all ages, not, "Ye shall be" (though that also is true), but, "Ye *are* saved through faith."

—from "Salvation by Faith"

Are saved. We are saved *now*. Our salvation isn't just something that will happen to us in the future, at the hour of our death—though John Wesley maintains that this also is certainly true—but our glorious salvation we *now* possess today. It is first and foremost a "present salvation."

Too often we're like the man who died in poverty with a mattress stuffed with money. We don't avail ourselves of all that pertains to our salvation today—we look for it as something to be enjoyed only in eternity. But eternal life begins the moment we believe and remains with us as we journey through life.

A man like John Wesley could only be sustained through his long decades of service by a faith that was *present*. And that same faith is available to us *today*. Let that faith form your life by freeing you from all guilt of sins past and the power of sin present.

This then is the salvation which is through faith, even in the present world: a salvation from sin, and the consequences of sin, both often expressed in the word *justification*; which, taken in the largest sense, implies a deliverance from guilt and punishment, by the atonement of Christ actually applied to the soul of the sinner now believing on Him, and a deliverance from the power of sin, through Christ *formed in his heart*.

—from "Salvation by Faith"

44

Believe

If you can believe, all things are possible to him who believes.

—Mark 9:23

ow does the Christian receive from God?
By faith. By believing.

Many times have I thought, many times have I spoke, many times have I wrote upon these words; and yet there appears to be a depth in them which I am in no wise able to fathom. Faith is, in one sense of the word, a divine conviction of God and of the things of God; in another, (nearly related to, yet not altogether the same) it is a divine conviction of the invisible and eternal world.

—from "On Faith," Sermon 122, 1872

God has chosen faith as the condition by which to save us, sanctify us, deliver us from evil, and bring us safely home to heaven.

But faith isn't just the entrance into God's family; it's the daily currency of His kingdom. Every day we are called to live by faith, not by sight. Our daily bread is supplied through faith. Our next breath is supplied by faith. Our loved ones are kept by faith.

Today is to be understood by faith. Nothing will happen today that God has not designed to be passed through by faith.

By this faith we are saved from all uneasiness of mind, from the anguish of a wounded spirit, from discontent, from fear and sorrow of heart, and from that inexpressible listlessness and weariness, both of the world and of ourselves, which we had so helplessly labored under for so many years, especially when we were out of hurry of the world and sunk into calm reflection.

—from "An Earnest Appeal to Men of Reason and Religion"

45

Meekness

Blessed are the meek,
For they shall inherit the earth.

—Matthew 5:5

They who are truly meek can clearly discern what is evil; and they can also suffer it. They are sensible of everything of this kind, but still meekness holds the reins. They are exceeding "zealous for the Lord of hosts;" but their zeal is always guided by knowledge, and tempered, in every thought, and word, and work, with the love of man, as well as the love of God. . . .

They do not desire to extinguish any of the passions which God has for wise ends implanted in their nature; but they have the mastery of all: They hold them all in subjection, and employ them only in subservience to those ends. And thus even the harsher and more unpleasing passions are applicable to the noblest purposes; even hatred, and anger, and fear, when engaged against sin, and regulated by faith and love, are as walls and fortifications to the soul, so that the wicked one cannot approach to hurt it.

—from "Upon Our Lord's Sermon on the Mount"

John Wesley brilliantly describes meekness as passions under control that are exercised against sin and *for* God. Christians are not a passionless people, but men and women who have put reins on their passion, thus able to employ them as necessary.

It's easy to spot those who have not learned meekness. Their zeal for God or religion is not under control; rather, it runs wild and burns like a forest fire, destroying all in its path.

True meekness is restorative. It builds, not destroys.

May God grant us the ability to so control our passions in His use.

Being taught of Him who was meek as well as lowly in heart, we shall then be enabled to "walk with all meekness;" being taught of Him who teacheth as never man taught, to be meek as well as lowly in heart. This implies not only a power over anger, but over all violent and turbulent passions.

It implies the having all our passions in due proportion; none of them either too strong or too weak; but all duly balanced with each other; all subordinate to reason; and reason directed by the Spirit of God. Let this equanimity govern your whole souls; that your thoughts may all flow in an even stream, and the uniform tenor of your words and actions be suitable thereto.

—from "Of the Church"

46

Hungering
after Righteousness

Blessed are those who hunger and thirst for righteousness,
For they shall be filled.

—Matthew 5:6

Hunger and thirst are the strongest of all our bodily appetites. In like manner this hunger in the soul, this thirst after the image of God, is the strongest of all our spiritual appetites, when it is once awakened in the heart: Yea, it swallows up all the rest in that one great desire,—to be renewed after the likeness of Him that created us.

—from "Upon the Sermon on the Mount"

A person who is full does not hunger. To be content with our own righteousness is to see no need of being filled with the manna of our Father's righteousness. We cannot stand before God in our own rags of righteousness. We must exchange them for His holiness. We must *hunger* for Him. The promise is that if we do so hunger, He will fill us—and we shall never again be famished.

Lord, increase our hunger and thirst for righteousness!

[Those who hunger and thirst for righteousness] shall be filled with the things which they long for; even with righteousness and true holiness. God shall satisfy them with the blessings of His goodness, with the felicity of His chosen.

He shall feed them with the bread of heaven, with the manna of His love. He shall give them to drink of His pleasures as out of the river, which he that drinketh of shall never thirst, only for more and more of the water of life.

—from "Upon the Sermon on the Mount"

Reason alone will convince every fair inquirer, that God "is a rewarder of them that diligently seek Him." This alone teaches him to say, "Doubtless there is a reward for the righteous."

—from "The Reward of the Righteous," Sermon 99, 1782

47

Now I Have
Lived a Day

All things have been delivered to Me by My Father, and no one knows the
Son except the Father. Nor does anyone know the Father except
the Son, and the one to whom the Son wills to reveal Him.

—Matthew 11:27

Have you ever had an experience when God's presence was so real, you knew you'd never forget it? For John Wesley, this awesome sense of God's nearness happened in December 1744. He writes:

In the evening, while I was reading prayers at Snowsfield, I found such light and strength as I never remember to have had before. I saw every thought as well as action or word, just as it was rising in my heart, and whether it was right before God, or tainted with pride or selfishness.

I waked the next morning, by the grace of God, in the same spirit; and about eight, being with two or three that believed in Jesus, I felt such an awe, and tender sense of the presence of God, as greatly confirmed me therein; so that God was before me all the day long. I sought and found Him in every place and could truly say, when I lay down at night, "now I have lived a day."

Such experiences are rare. Other than his Aldersgate experience, in all his eighty-seven years, Wesley records very little about his private experiences of God's presence, though he does mention occasions during his preaching when God's presence was manifestly felt. But God was no less with him every other day of his life than on that December day in 1744.

You may never know the presence of God in the way Wesley felt him on that particular day. That's up to God. But you *can* know Him by faith in His fullness just as if such an experience was yours.

Simply acknowledge His promise that He will never leave nor forsake you. That certainty is yours by faith. At the end of this day or any day, you can surely say with confidence, "Now I have lived a day."

In January, 1738, I expressed my desire in these words:—
O grant that nothing in my soul
May dwell but thy pure love alone!
O may thy love possess me whole,
My Joy, my treasure, and my crown!
Strange flames far from my heart remove,
My every act, word, thought be love!

—from John Wesley's journal, May, 1765

48

Ten Thousand Cares

. . . casting all your care upon Him, for He cares for you.
—1 Peter 5:7

I had often wondered at myself (and sometimes mentioned it to others) that ten thousand cares, of various kinds, were no more weight and burden to my mind than ten thousand hairs were to my head.

Perhaps I began to ascribe something of this to my own strength. And thence it might be that on Sunday that strength was withheld, and I felt what it was to be troubled about many things. One and another hurrying me continually, it seized upon my spirit more and more till I found it absolutely necessary to fly for my life, and that without delay. So the next day, Monday, I took horse and rode away from Bristol.

Between Bath and Bristol I was earnestly desired to turn aside and call at the house of a poor man, William Shalwood. I found him and his wife sick in one bed, and with small hopes of the recovery of either. Yet (after prayer) I believed they would "not die, but live, and declare the loving-kindness of the Lord." The next time I called he was sitting downstairs, and his wife able to go abroad.

As soon as we came into the house at Bristol, my soul was lightened of her load, of that insufferable weight which had lain upon my mind, more or less, for several days. On Sunday, several of our friends from Wales and other parts joined with us in the great sacrifice of thanksgiving. And every day we found more and more cause to praise God and to give Him thanks for His still increasing benefits.

—Saturday, January 5, 1745

John Wesley *did* have an occasional bout with anxiety when he "felt what it was to be troubled about many things." It was rare, but it did happen.

What are your cares today? What weighs heavily on your mind? Your children? Your spouse? Your job? Finances? Health? Temptations?

God has time for each care we can utter. And He painstakingly assures us that He will see to every matter that troubles us.

We humble ourselves, O Lord of heaven and earth, before thy glorious majesty. We acknowledge thy eternal power, wisdom, goodness, and truth; and desire to render thee unfeigned thanks for all the benefits you pourest upon us, but above all, for thine inestimable love in the redemption of the world by our Lord Jesus Christ.

—from "Prayers for Families"

49

The Perfect Friend

There is a friend who sticks closer than a brother.
—Proverbs 18:24

I think we've all been in the situation where we've overheard someone near us using profane language. What was our response? Surely we cringe at such behavior. But John Wesley had a more direct response—and it's noteworthy the way he approaches the offender. He appeals to the sense of friendship that God has for sinners, including those who revile Him.

> At Darlington (it being the fair day) we could scarce find a place to hide our head. At length we got into a little inn, but were obliged to be in a room where there was another set of company, some of whom were cursing and swearing much.
>
> Before we went away, I stepped to them, and asked, "Do you think yourselves that this kind of talking is right?" One of them warmly replied, "Sir, we have said nothing which we have need to be ashamed of." I said, "Have you not need to be ashamed of disobliging your best friend? And is not God

the best friend you have?" They stared first at me, and then at one another; but no man answered a word.

—Monday, April 14, 1745

The gospel in its simplest form is that God has condescended to become the friend of sinners. Jesus exemplified this truth to the extent that many criticized Him for hanging out with the lowest of the low. In fact, Jesus was accused of being a drunkard and a glutton himself. That didn't bother Jesus. He knew His mission was not to the righteous, but to the unrighteous—to *us*.

John Wesley confronted blasphemers who were no doubt oblivious to the fact that their cursing was an affront to the best friend they had: their Savior.

Are you in need of a best friend? One who sticks closer than a loving brother? One who knows you better than anyone else—and still sticks by you?

Being a Christian is to be a dear friend of God. Is there really any other person who can do a better job at friendship than Jesus?

He can be trusted. He can be confided in. He can be everything that the best human friend cannot be.

Today, contemplate what it means to have God as your dearest friend. It's an awesome thought.

Whatever enemies you have, it is enough that you have a Friend who is mightier than them all. O let Him reign in your heart alone!

—from a letter to Dorothy Furly, June 14, 1757

50

The Brevity of Life

For what is your life? It is even a vapor that appears
for a little time and then vanishes away.

—James 4:14

We've all asked the following question John Wesley posed in the Thursday, March 19, 1747 entry in his journal:

I considered, "What would I do now, if I was sure I had but two days to live?" All outward things are settled to my wish; the Houses at Bristol, Kingswood, and Newcastle are safe; the deeds whereby they are conveyed to the Trustees took place on the 5th instant; my Will is made . . . what have I more to do, but to commend my soul to my merciful and faithful Creator?

In his fifty-first year, Wesley thought he might be dying. This time he was prompted to write his epitaph, which was to read,

Here lieth the body of John Wesley,
A brand plucked out the burning;
Who died of a consumption in the fifty-first year of his age,

Not leaving, after his debts are paid, ten pounds behind him:
God be merciful to me, an unprofitable servant!

Both times, Wesley's affairs were in order. He was ready to lay down his life at his Lord's bidding and enter into eternity. Little did he know that he had decades of life still ahead of him, years filled with extreme productivity and ministry.

None of us know how much time we have left. It's all in God's hands. Perhaps, indeed, some of us have only a very short time left. What then? How would we live if we were given a glimpse of how much time remains for us?

Some of us may have as much as half a century still ahead of us. Much can be accomplished in those years—if the decision is made to live with our eyes so focused on eternity that we can safely say with Wesley that we have commended our souls to a merciful and faithful Creator.

And that is the secret of treasuring our time left on earth—to live each day in the full assurance that God is with us.

In order to redeem the time; Improve the present moment. Buy up every opportunity of growing in grace, or of doing good. Let not the thought of receiving more grace tomorrow, make you negligent of today.

—from "Satan's Devices"

51

Inward Prayer

*Likewise the Spirit also helps in our weaknesses. For we do not
know what we should pray for as we ought, but the Spirit Himself makes
intercession for us with groanings which cannot be uttered.*

—Romans 8:26

Ever felt like you just didn't know how to pray about a matter? Or
that you couldn't even muster up the strength to pray? Sometimes
we have such enormous burdens that we just don't have words.

But even then—*especially* then—the Holy Spirit is able to pray
through us. He knows the will of God. He *is* God. We don't have to
bow our heads, fold our hands, or get on our knees to pray effectively.
The Spirit can pray through us while in any position or engaged in any
activity. The very desire of our heart can be a prayer.

> All that a Christian does, even in eating and sleeping, is
> prayer, when it is done in simplicity, according to the order of
> God, without either adding to or diminishing from it by His
> own choice. Prayer continues in the desire of the heart,
> though the understanding be employed on outward things. . . .
> God only requires of His adult children, that their hearts be
> truly purified, and that they offer Him continually the wishes
> and vows that naturally spring from perfect love. For these

desires, being the genuine fruits of love, are the most perfect prayers that can spring from it.

—from *A Plain Account of Christian Perfection*

Our very desires can become prayers to God. Wesley only cautions that those desires must spring from a heart of pure love: "For these desires, being the genuine fruits of love, are the most perfect prayers that can spring from it."

In souls filled with love, the desire to please God is a continual prayer.

—from *A Plain Account of Christian Perfection*

52

Fellowship

For as the body is one and has many members, but all the members
of that one body, being many, are one body, so also is Christ.
—1 Corinthians 12:12

Possibly one of the greatest disappointments of John Wesley's life was that his society should spin off into what would become another denomination. During his early years, Wesley was determined to see his ministry accomplished through the Anglican Church, which he loved. But it was not to be. Neither the Anglicans wanted what the "Methodists" had to offer, nor did the Methodists want to compromise in order to become acceptable to the Anglican leadership.

A story has been widely circulated that Wesley dreamed he was ushered to the gates of hell. There he asked, "Are there any Presbyterians here?" "Yes!" was the reply. He then asked, "Are there any Baptists? Any Episcopalians? Any Methodists?" The answer was yes each time.

Much distressed, Wesley was then escorted to the gates of heaven where he asked the same question, and the answer was no.

Much astonished, Wesley asked, "Who then is inside?"

The answer came back, "There are only Christians here."

Since Wesley's day, there have been many movements that have evolved into yet more denominations. And yet, through all the seeming divisions among believers, there *has* to be unity in the essentials of the faith. And beyond the common ground of our core Christian beliefs, there is an even deeper unity to be enjoyed by Christians—the recognition that there is really only *one* body of Christ. Many members—but one body.

Throughout his ministry, God gifted John Wesley with faithful colleagues who "got it." They knew what God was doing through Wesley, and they knew they had a part to play. They were needed, and they knew it.

A few years before his dramatic spiritual experience at Aldersgate, Wesley, in his search for truth, met a wise man who told him that if he wanted to serve God and to reach heaven, he must either *find* companions along the way or *make* them. "The Bible knows nothing of solitary religion," the man told Wesley. And Wesley never forgot those words.

Nor should we. We need all our brothers and sisters in Christ to do the work at hand.

53

More than
a Conqueror

*Yet in all these things we are more than conquerors through Him who
loved us. For I am persuaded that neither death nor life, nor angels nor
principalities nor powers, nor things present nor things to come, nor
height nor depth, nor any other created thing, shall be able to separate
us from the love of God which is in Christ Jesus our Lord.*

—Romans 8:37–39

O ne of few impossibilities in this universe is this: nothing can
separate us from the love of God. Nothing! It was this great
truth that caused the Apostle Paul to proclaim every Christian as more
than a conqueror. It's what caused John Wesley to call us "gainers for
ever and ever" as he wrote:

> If we suffer from the mean habitation of the immortal spirit;
> if pain, sickness, and numberless other afflictions beside, to
> which we should not otherwise have been liable, assault us on
> every side, and at length bear us down into the dust of death;
> what are we losers by this? Losers! No, "In all these things we
> are more than conquerors, through him that loved us."
>
> Come on then, disease, weakness, pain,—afflictions, in
> the language of men. Shall we not be infinite gainers by
> them? Gainers for ever and ever!
>
> —from "The Heavenly Treasure in Earthen Vessels"

It's one thing to endure affliction—but Wesley sees every obstacle that comes our way as an opportunity to live as conquerors. Likewise, temptations are merely minor assaults over which we may surely be victorious.

To be entirely devoted to God is to be given the crown of the conqueror.

Always remember the essence of Christian holiness is simplicity and purity; one design, one desire—entire devotion to God. But this admits of a thousand degrees and variations, and certainly it will be proved by a thousand temptations; but in all these things you shall be more than conqueror.

—from a letter to Miss March, April 14, 1771

54

Human Frailty

Forgive, and you will be forgiven.
—Luke 6:37

ohn Wesley knew about human frailty. Although a highly accomplished man, Wesley perceived his own shortcomings—all the more so the older he got. He had also seen the failure of others close to him: his estranged wife, many of the men he mentored who eventually turned to other doctrines, and, of course, the many men and women who stood firmly against him, even to the point of violence. But he learned to be a good forgiver of wrongs committed against him.

In a January 25, 1757, letter to Samuel Furly, a young associate he hoped to see ordained as a parish priest, Wesley closed the personal note with a warning about the young man's temper. He cautioned the lad to make allowances for others, as he himself had learned to do, by saying, "The longer I live, the larger allowances I make for human infirmities. I exact more from myself and less from others. Go thou and do likewise!"

Whose human frailty will we be called on to overlook today? Rest assured, if you deal with human beings, you *will* encounter human weakness in the form of rudeness, insensitivity, ignorance, pride, and a host of other manifestations of human nature. To allow ahead of time for the frailties of others is to head off trouble.

And just remember, someone else today may be needing to overlook *your* frailties.

A noted British general once told Wesley, "I'll never forgive!" To which Wesley replied, "Then, Sir, you had better never sin."

55

The Springs
of Happiness

For my people have committed two evils:
They have forsaken Me, the fountain of living waters,
And hewn themselves cisterns—broken cisterns than can hold no water.

—Jeremiah 2:13

What's the source of so much of our dissatisfaction? Why aren't we more content? It's because we do two things wrong: First, we don't come to God *first* in all of our wants, trials, and maladies. Second, we subtly or openly seek satisfaction elsewhere; we hew out cisterns, broken cisterns that can hold no water.

> Many indeed think of being happy with God in heaven; but being happy in God on earth never entered into their thoughts. The less so, because from the time they come into the world, they are surrounded with idols. Such, in turns, are all "the things that are seen," (whereas God is not seen,) which all promise an happiness independent of God.
>
> — from "The Unity of the Divine Being," Sermon 114

Dorothy Furly was one of many dear friends of John Wesley to whom he often wrote and visited. In this September 25, 1757, letter, Wesley comforts her as she walked a "thorny path."

It is plain God sees it best for you frequently to walk in a thorny path. By this means He aims at destroying your pride of heart and breaking your stubborn will. You have had large experience that there is no substantial or lasting happiness but in Him. O be true to yourself and to your own experience! Do not seek it where it cannot be found. Hew out to yourself no more broken cisterns, but let all the springs of your happiness be in Him.

Miss Furly's path became even thornier in the years ahead. In 1764 she married John Downes, a Methodist preacher who died suddenly in 1774. She remained a widow until her death at age seventy-six in 1807. Did she ever heed the advice Wesley had given her in the letter above? Yes, apparently so. Charles Wesley visited the bereaved widow shortly after her husband's death. He reported,

She surprised me and all who saw her. So supported, so calm, so resigned! A faithful friend received her into his house. She had one sixpence in the world, and no more! But her Maker is her husband!

Dorothy Furly had learned not to seek happiness where it cannot be found. Oh that we each could say the same. May we forsake the broken cisterns that can never satisfy, and turn to the One who wishes to become to us a fountain of living water!

56

Persecution

*Blessed are you when they revile and persecute you, and say all kinds
of evil against you falsely for My sake. Rejoice and be exceedingly
glad, for great is your reward in heaven, for so they persecuted the
prophets who were before you.*

—Matthew 5:11–12

The history of the great men and women of God is a history of
persecution. John Wesley was no exception. Even before he
came to a full understanding of his salvation at Aldersgate, his desire
for the Lord brought him jeers, pranks, and even violence.

After his conversion, matters only became worse. Wesley often
aroused intense anger in his listeners. He was beaten, pummeled with
rocks, slandered, kicked, and more than once barely escaped with his
life. Not only was Wesley persecuted, but his followers, the early
Methodists, were also met with hatred. Their lives were threatened,
their homes were damaged, their reputations destroyed.

One such incident happened in Wednesbury. Months after his
successful preaching ministry there, Wesley heard stories of intense
persecution against his followers and returned to the community to
see what he could do.

At noon he preached to the throngs with little reaction. But that
night, an angry mob surrounded the house where he was staying and
yelled, "Bring out the minister. We will have the minister!"

Wesley met with his accusers and won over many of his detractors—but not all. A mob of two to three hundred citizens escorted him to first one magistrate and then another; the angry men hoping to find a sympathetic ear in the courts. At the second village, Walsal, a fight erupted among Wesley's defenders and yet a new mob of accusers from the locals there.

Wesley was fiercely attacked. One man tried to bludgeon Wesley, but he ducked in time—only to be met with a blow to the mouth, drawing blood. When Wesley tried to speak to the mob, the answer was, "No! Knock his brains out! Kill him! Crucify the dog!"

But Wesley prevailed in being heard, speaking with authority—and no fear. Many of his tormentors were cut to the quick, their hearts broken by the prayer Wesley uttered. Their leader, a noted fighter, swore to guard Wesley with his life. As the mob dispersed, Wesley was escorted by his former foe back to his lodgings at Wednesbury. The row was over, and the Methodist movement grew in the region.

God brought me safe to Wednesbury; I having lost only one flap of my waistcoat and a little skin from one of my hands.

— from John Wesley's journal

57

Pure Love

Then one of the scribes came, and having heard them reasoning together, perceiving that He had answered them well, asked Him, "Which is the first commandment of all?"

Jesus answered him, "The first of all the commandments is: 'Hear, O Israel, the Lord our God, the Lord is one. And you shall love the Lord your God with all your heart, with all your soul, with all your mind, and with all your strength.' This is the first commandment. And the second, like it, is this: 'You shall love your neighbor as yourself.' There is no other commandment greater than these."

—Mark 12:28–31

In 1759, John Wesley published his classic *Thoughts on Christian Perfection*. The principles he laid out in this practical work were not simply random thoughts of the great evangelist. Instead, he noted that he had believed and lived by these tenets for many years previous to their publication.

Set down in question and answer form, the very first entry explains exactly what Christian perfection is.

Q: *What is Christian perfection?*

A: The loving God with all our heart, mind, soul, and strength. This implies, that no wrong temper, none contrary to love, remains in the soul; and that all the thoughts, words, and actions, are governed by pure love.

Pure love, Wesley maintained, is the governing force that enables the true Christian to live the life of perfection that we each hunger for.

The rest of Wesley's famous tract further explains the many aspects of perfection and how each of us may live it fully. But it's upon this firm foundation of "pure love" that the entire Christian life stands—or falls—if love is not present.

Pure love of God must be evidenced by fulfilling the second commandment Jesus proclaimed as the greatest: loving others as we love ourselves.

The perfect Christian, then, is the perfect lover of God and of others.

Day by day we are each given opportunities—some perhaps in great disguise—to love others in practical ways. When we do show God's love toward others, we are expressing the perfection of God.

How can perfect love be seen in you today? There is no doubt God will provide at least one golden opportunity. He always does. Watch for it and apply perfect love.

Without this [love], all we know, all we believe, all we do, all we suffer, will profit us nothing in the great day of accounts.

—from "The More Excellent Way"

58

On Singing

Is anyone cheerful? Let him sing psalms.

—James 5:13

Nothing was too small to escape John Wesley's notice. He had opinions on just about everything that pertained to the worship of God—even singing. His "Directions for Singing" is an exhortation to the correct way to worship God through congregational singing. Here are a few of his directions:

Sing all. See that you join with the congregation as frequently as you can. Let not a single degree of weakness or weariness hinder you. If it is a cross to you, take it up, and you will find it a blessing.

Sing lustily and with good courage. Beware of singing as if you were half dead, or half asleep; but lift up your voice with strength. Be no more afraid of your voice now, nor more ashamed of its being heard, then when you sung the songs of Satan.

Sing modestly. Do not bawl, so as to be heard above or distinct from the rest of the congregation, that you may not destroy the harmony; but strive to unite your voices together, so as to make one clear melodious sound.

Above all sing spiritually. Have an eye to God in every word you sing. Aim at pleasing Him more than yourself, or any other creature. In order to do this attend strictly to the sense of what you sing, and see that your heart is not carried away with the sound, but offered to God continually; so shall your singing be such as the Lord will approve here, and reward you when He cometh in the clouds of heaven.

—from John Wesley's *Select Hymns,* 1761

Singing as a vital part of worship was so important to John Wesley that he records in his journal his disappointment in hearing only a few vibrant voices:

Mr. Smyth read prayers, and gave out the hymns, which were sung by fifteen or twenty fine singers; the rest of the congregation listening with much attention, and as much devotion as they would have done to an opera. But is this Christian worship? Or ought it even to be suffered in a Christian Church?

—from John Wesley's journal, 1787

59

Sin in the Believer

Therefore do not let sin reign in your mortal body,
that you should obey it in its lusts.

—Romans 6:12

"But can Christ be in the same heart where sin is?"
Undoubtedly He can; otherwise it never could be
saved therefrom. Where the sickness is, there is the Physician.

—from "On Sin in Believers"

Christ, the Good Physician, attends the bedside of every sinner.
He doesn't cast us out when we bring our sin to Him with a contrite
heart. No, He takes way our sin and walks with us through our fight
against sin. Sometimes we forget that Jesus was tempted at all points
as we are. There is no temptation you face that Christ himself did not
face. Christ was and *is* the Friend of Sinners.

He is *your* friend.

Christ indeed cannot reign, where sin reigns; neither will he
dwell where any sin is allowed. But He is and dwells in the
heart of every believer, who is fighting against all sin;

although it be not yet purified, according to the purification of the sanctuary.

—from "On Sin in Believers"

Don't be discouraged by the fact that you still sin. Instead, be encouraged that you have a Savior from your sin. Do not look at your sin, but at your Savior and receive from Him all the grace to overcome.

God loves you: therefore love and obey Him. Christ dies for you: therefore die to sin. Christ is risen: therefore rise in the image of God. Christ liveth evermore: therefore live to God, till you live with Him in glory. So we preached; and so you believed. This is the scriptural way, the Methodist way, the true way.

—from a letter to Ebenezer Blackwell, December 20, 1751

So that no man sins because he has not grace, but because He does not use the grace which he hath.

—from "On Working Out Our Own Salvation"

60

Pride

Do you see a man wise in his own eyes?
There is more hope for a fool than for him.

—Proverbs 26:12

The Methodist "advices" were published as a tract in 1762, under the title of "Cautions and Directions Given to the Greatest Professors in the Methodist Societies." The motto was,

"Set the false witnesses aside, yet hold the truth for ever fast."

Q. *What is the First advice that you would give them?*

A. Watch and pray continually against pride. If God has cast it out, see that it enter no more: It is full as dangerous as desire. And you may slide back into it unawares; especially if you think there is no danger of it.

How has pride affected us? One gauge is by how we react when proven right or wrong in a matter. If we are right, we beam with pride—and yet our attitude betrays any evidence of humility. If we are wrong, we may resent having been shown up as somehow less astute than someone else.

A test of pride, then can be summed up by the ease with which we can say things like,

- I'm sorry.

- Would you help me?

- I was wrong and you were right.

- I misjudged you.

- I love you just the way you are.

Wesley counsels us to beware of pride when we know we are wrong. Acknowledging our mistakes shows we have no need to be in the right. It shows we can handle humility—as well we should. Each of us has much to be humble about.

Be always ready to own any fault you have been in. If you have at any time thought, spoke, or acted wrong, be not backward to acknowledge it. Never dream that this will hurt the cause of God; no, it will further it. Be therefore open and frank, when you are taxed with anything; do not seek either to evade or disguise it; but let it appear just as it is, and you will thereby not hinder, but adorn, the gospel.

—from *A Plain Account of Christian Perfection*

61

Enthusiasm

Beloved, do not believe every spirit, but test the spirits, whether they are of God; because many false prophets have gone out into the world. By this you know the Spirit of God: Every spirit that confesses that Jesus Christ has come in the flesh is of God, and every spirit that does not confess that Jesus Christ has come in the flesh is not of God.

—1 John 4:1–3

John Wesley continues his Methodist advices with what may be, at first glance, a strange consideration:

Q. *What is the Second advice which you would give them?*

A. Beware of that daughter of pride, enthusiasm. O keep at the utmost distance from it! Give no place to a heated imagination. Do not hastily ascribe things to God. Do not easily suppose dreams, voices, impressions, visions, or revelations to be from God. They may be from Him. They may be from nature. They may be from the devil. Therefore, "believe not every spirit, but try the spirits whether they be of God."

John Wesley understood the human condition. We are easily swayed by our enthusiasms or feelings, even to the extent of allowing them to drive our spiritual life—and that to our own harm.

For Wesley, it was God's written Word that was the only arbiter of truth. A false sense of enthusiasm could easily wage war with godly reason. Further, he saw feelings as an instrument through which Satan himself might lead a believer astray.

> Some have been ignorant of this device of Satan. They have left off searching the Scriptures. They said, "God writes all the Scriptures on my heart. Therefore, I have no need to read it." Others thought they had not so much need of hearing, and so grew slack in attending the morning preaching. O take warning, you who are concerned herein! You have listened to the voice of a stranger. Fly back to Christ, and keep in the good old way, which was "once delivered to the saints . . ."
>
> —from "The Advices"

Wesley cautions us that one sign of false enthusiasm is the expectation that everything in the spiritual life should come easy for us—with no discipline on our part. He writes,

> One general inlet to enthusiasm is, expecting the end without the means; the expecting knowledge, for instance, without searching the Scriptures, and consulting the children of God; the expecting spiritual strength without constant prayer, and steady watchfulness; the expecting any blessing without hearing the word of God at every opportunity.
>
> —from *A Plain Account of Christian Perfection*

I say yet again, beware of enthusiasm.

> —from "The Advices"

62

Fasting

. . . in weariness and toil, in sleeplessness often, in hunger and thirst,
in fastings often, in cold and nakedness . . .

—2 Corinthians 11:27

Is the spiritual discipline of fasting still valuable today? Yes! Nowhere in the Bible do we find God changing His mind about calling His people to fasting under certain circumstances.

John Wesley enhanced his prayer life with fasting and urged others to do so also.

> But of all the means of grace there is scarce any concerning which men have run into greater extremes, than that of . . . religious fasting. How have some exalted this beyond all Scripture and reason;—and others utterly disregarded it; as it were revenging themselves by undervaluing as much as the former had overvalued it!
>
> Those have spoken of it, as if it were all in all; if not the end itself, yet infallibly connected with it: These, as if it were just nothing, as if it were a fruitless labour, which had no relation at all thereto. Whereas it is certain the truth lies between them both. It is not all, nor yet is it nothing. It is not the end,

but it is a precious means thereto; a means which God himself has ordained, and in which therefore, when it is duly used, He will surely give us His blessing.

Fasting in conjunction with prayer can accomplish much.

And with fasting let us always join fervent prayer, pouring out our whole souls before God, confessing our sins with all their aggravations, humbling ourselves under His mighty hand, laying open before Him all our wants, all our guiltiness and helplessness.

This is a season for enlarging our prayers, both in behalf of ourselves and of our brethren. Let us now bewail the sins of our people; and cry aloud for the city of our God, that the Lord may build up Zion, and cause His face to shine on her desolations. Thus, we may observe, the men of God, in ancient times always joined prayer and fasting together.

—from "Upon Our Lord's Sermon on The Mount"

God will hearken to the prayer that goeth not out of feigned lips; especially when fasting, is joined there with.

—from a letter, November 24, 1785

63

A Dozen Oysters

Where is the wise? Where is the scribe? Where is the disputer of this
age? Has not God made foolish the wisdom of this world?

—1 Corinthians 1:20

It's interesting to note how clearly God prefers that which most people reject. The Jews had expected their messiah to come as a conquering king, not a babe born in a stable. The Pharisees rejected the message of grace because it permitted sinners an entrance to God's kingdom. And the high churchmen just couldn't handle the simplicity of both Wesley's message and his unseemly methods.

One of Wesley's unlearned preachers was preaching to a crowd on Luke 19:21, "Lord, I feared thee, because thou art an austere man." The man didn't know the word *austere*, and so he assumed the text was referring to an *oyster* man. So during his message, the man recounted the work of those "oyster men" who retrieve oysters from the seabed. He told how the diver plunges into the icy water, away from his comfortable air-filled environment. Then he gropes in the dark against the sharp edges of the shells, cutting his hands in the process. Once he has the oyster, he then surfaces and is back to his familiar home, with air and warmth. In his bloody hands, he bears the triumphant prize he had sought, the precious oyster. Just so, the preacher said, Christ left His home in heaven to be submerged in the foreign and repellant environment of earth in order to save men and women and bring them back to heaven.

Yes, the man said, Jesus like the oyster man, gained the prize he sought through the blood spilt in the process.

The illustration resulted in twelve men converted to Christ that night. But later, one of the more knowledgeable men complained about the wrongness of the illustration and muttered that such unlearned men should not be allowed to preach. But Wesley's smiling response was, "Never mind, the Lord got a dozen oysters tonight."

We must never be ashamed or embarrassed by the ordinariness and simplicity of our faith. Because behind it all, there lies a beautiful mystery that shall one day be revealed.

I spent an agreeable hour at a concert of my nephews. But I was a little out of my element among Lords and Ladies. I love plain music and plain company best.

—from John Wesley's journal, 1781

64

Magnificence
of Thought

It is the glory of God to conceal a matter,
But the glory of kings is to search out a matter.

—Proverbs 25:2

The great lesson that our blessed Lord [reminds us] . . . is that God is in all things, and that we are to see the Creator in the glass of every creature; that we should use and look upon nothing as separate from God, which indeed is a kind of practical atheism; but with a true magnificence of thought survey heaven and earth and all that is therein as contained by God in the hollow of His hand, who by His intimate presence holds them all in being, who pervades and activates the whole created frame, and is in a true sense the soul of the universe.

—from "Sermon on the Mount III," 1748

John Wesley's hunger (and his insatiable curiosity) for God and His truth compelled him to look for the workings of God in places many Christians never venture. To Wesley, God could be seen in all things—in man, in nature, in science, in medicine, in philosophy, in artistic expression—and in all these endeavors, Wesley ventured boldly forth.

Wesley was extremely well read on these and other subjects. He could enter a rousing debate and offer points of persuasion that silenced his opponents.

In his frequent travels on horseback, Wesley could often be seen with a book perched before him. In that sense, Wesley was an early "multi-tasker." And in each of his forays into new fields of learning, Wesley did indeed find God.

In like manner, we should never be afraid to pursue the curiosities that God has planted in us. God conceals many matters from us, but it is "the glory of kings" to search out those hidden matters, to truly *see* the hand of God in every aspect of life.

Today, God may appear to you in an unexpected place. You may learn something new and immediately see the hand of God revealed. You may remember something from your past that has long been a mystery and then all is clear. You see from God's perspective what He was doing all along. Or you may hear a song, see a painting, or read a book and be at once in God's presence.

No matter what field of endeavor you find yourself in—science, medicine, philosophy, astronomy, quilting, painting, writing, music— look for the hand of God, and you will find Him, for He has wrought all things.

How small a part of this great work of God is man able to understand! But it is our duty to contemplate what He has wrought, and to understand as much of it as we are able.

—from "God's Approbation of His Works," 1782

65

Religion and Reason

Therefore gird up the loins of your mind . . .
—1 Peter 1:13

It is a fundamental principle with us [Methodists] that to renounce reason is to renounce religion, that religion and reason go hand in hand, and that all irrational religion is false religion.

—from a letter to Dr. Rutherford, March 28, 1768

One of the many gifts God has given us is the ability to think. Though this gift has been affected by sin, when we were redeemed, so was our mind. Scripture tells us we now have the mind of Christ. We have a *sound* mind. Our reasoning abilities can go hand in hand with our faith.

"If reason be against a man, a man will always be against reason." This has been confirmed by the experience of all ages. Very many have been the instances of it in the Christian as well as the heathen world; yea, and that in the earliest times. Even then there were not wanting well-meaning men who, not having much reason themselves, imagined that reason was of no use in religion; yea, rather, that it was a hinderance to it. And there has not been wanting a succession of men who have believed and asserted the same thing. But never was there a greater number of these in the Christian Church, at least in Britain, than at this day.

—from "The Case of Reason Impartially Considered," Sermon 70

It is highly reasonable to be a person of faith, and it is quite unreasonable to reject faith. As the Psalmist reminds us, "the fool has said in his heart 'there is no God.'"

Those who reject a reasonable faith are the most likely to struggle with such values as love, joy, patience—what we know as the fruit of the Spirit. True happiness is found in reason and faith, the marriage of the redeemed mind and the redeemed heart.

True religion is the highest reason. It is indeed wisdom, virtue, and happiness in one.

—from a letter to the editor of *Lloyd's Evening Post,* December 1, 1760

66

Little Crosses

That is why we never give up. Though our bodies are dying, our
spirits are being renewed every day. For our present troubles are
quite small and won't last very long. Yet they produce for us an
immeasurably great glory that will last forever!

—2 Corinthians 4:16–17, NLT

Like each of us, John Wesley did not live a life without affliction. And also like many of us, one of Wesley's severest afflictions came from his family affairs—specifically from his troubled marriage. Against the advice of many close to him, including his brother, Charles, Wesley married a wealthy widow and reaped three decades of remorse. Interestingly, just a short time earlier, Wesley had written a tract commending the single life for Christians such as himself. Twice before he had been wounded by the sudden marriage of a young woman he loved to another suitor. He really should have known better.

But then he met Mary Vazeille, a successful merchant's widow, who had a handsome inheritance from her husband, and four children. She was an attractive woman, seven years younger than Wesley and seemed to be a pious woman. Shortly after their introduction, the two were wed.

It didn't take long for Wesley to realize that the marriage would have bitter results for both of them. The new Mrs. Wesley resented her husband's ministry with its long trips and often unbearable lodgings. She loved comfort more than she loved John. Several times she simply gave up and left her husband—and in 1771 she left for good. Though the couple was married for thirty years, they never saw each other for the last ten years of Mrs. Wesley's life. In her will, Mrs. Wesley left a gold ring to her husband, and all the rest of her property went to her son.

In retrospect, Wesley's marriage seems like the colossal mistake of his life—and perhaps it was. And yet, even in those troubled years, God was able to continue to use Wesley in a mighty way. This was a "little cross" that proved his mettle.

We each have such little crosses. Perhaps, like Wesley, it's a difficult marriage relationship. Or a job. Or health concerns. Or financial worries. And yet no matter which little crosses are to be ours, God's grace brings us through.

What a blessing it is to have these little crosses, that we may try what spirit we are of. We could not live in continual sunshine. It would dry up all the grace of God that is in us.

—from a letter to Ebenezer Blackwell, April 29, 1755

67

Do the
Right Thing

Bear fruits worthy of repentance.

—Matthew 3:8

J ohn Wesley wasn't afraid to stand up for what was right, even if his was an unpopular opinion. The topic of slavery is a perfect example. Wesley despised the loathsome buying and selling of other human beings, and both wrote and spoke openly in support of the abolition of slavery. Here's a sample of his passion on this isue:

> Are you a man? Then you should have a human heart. But have you indeed? What is your heart made of? Is there no such principle as compassion there? Do you never feel another's pain? Have you no sympathy, no sense of human woe, no pity for the miserable? When you saw the flowing eyes, the heaving breasts, or the bleeding sides and tortured limbs of your fellow-creatures, was you a stone, or a brute? Did you look upon them with the eyes of a tiger?
>
> When you squeezed the agonizing creatures down in the ship, or when you threw their poor mangled remains into the sea, had you no relenting? Did not one tear drop from your eye,

one sigh escape from your breast? Do you feel no relenting now?

Today resolve, God being your helper, to escape for your life. Regard not money! All that a man hath will he give for his life! Whatever you lose, lose not your soul: Nothing can countervail that loss. Immediately quit the horrid trade: At all events, be an honest man.

—from *Thoughts Upon Slavery*, 1774

Think about issues today that might be modern day versions of the slavery issue. Does your opinion match God's opinion? Or is it shaped more by contemporary thought? We must be sure to *know* right from wrong—and then we must work to promote that which is right. But be aware: doing so is not always the popular position.

Wesley prayed:

Arise, and help these that have no helper, whose blood is spilt upon the ground like water! Are not these also the work of thine own hands, the purchase of thy Son's blood? Stir them up to cry unto thee in the land of their captivity; and let their complaint come up before thee; let it enter into thy ears! Make even those that lead them away captive to pity them, and turn their captivity as the rivers in the south. O burst thou all their chains in sunder; more especially the chains of their sins! Thou Saviour of all, make them free, that they may be free indeed!

—from *Thoughts Upon Slavery*, 1774

Seeing the Prize

Beloved, let us love one another, for love is of God; and everyone who loves
is born of God and knows God. He who does not love does not know God, for
God is love. In this the love of God was manifested toward us, that
God has sent His only begotten Son into the world, that we might live
through Him. In this is love, not that we loved God, but that He loved
us and sent His Son to be the propitiation for our sins. Beloved, if
God so loved us, we also ought to love one another.

—1 John 4:7–11

As a young man, John Wesley had read the mystics and other Christian writers who had preceded him: Thomas a'Kempis's *The Imitation of Christ*, Jeremy Taylor's *Holy Living and Dying*, and the works of William Law. Of the former, he declared it too ascetic. But Wesley's extensive reading of the mystics did open a new world to Wesley. He wrote, "I began to alter the whole form of my conversation and to set about in earnest upon a new life. I set apart an hour or two a day for religious retirement; I communicated every week; I watched against all sin, whether in word or deed."

But like all Christians, he found it difficult to find God's peace through mere religious exercise, lacking the grace he would later find. Where asceticism failed, the love of God won him over. He discovered that it was the simplicity of love that could accomplish in him what the mystics could not. They were deep, but the gospel was simple. And what a great secret was there to be found in grace, as opposed to law.

It is indeed God's love demonstrated in His grace, not religious exercises, that nourishes the Christian life. At length, he rejected the works of William Law, the man who had been most influential in his early spiritual development. He simply discovered that there was a difference in the practical theology he found in the Bible as opposed to the mystical writings of his early mentors.

What he wanted was a Christianity that worked in real life.

I exchanged the Mystic writers for the scriptural.

—letter to the editor of the *London Chronicle,* September 17, 1760

69

Remembering
the Poor

*And when James, Cephas, and John, who seemed to be pillars,
perceived the grace that had been given to me, they gave me and Barnabas
the right hand of fellowship, that we should go to the Gentiles and they
to the circumcised. They desired only that we should remember
the poor, the very thing which I also was eager to do.*

—Galatians 2:9–10

Regarding the poor, John Wesley believed that it was the duty of
his societies to go to the poor—not wait for the poor to come
to them. Just as Jesus came to seek and save the lost, so too did
Wesley see the duty of Christians to expressly be attentive to the poor.
To one society matron, he wrote,

> Do not confine your conversation to gentle and elegant people.
> I should like this as well as you do. But I cannot discover a
> precedent for it in the life of our Lord, or any of His Apostles.
> My dear friend, let you and I walk as He walked. . . . I want
> you to converse more, abundantly more, with the poorest of
> the people, who, if they have not taste, have souls, which you
> may forward on their way to heaven. And they have (many of
> them) faith, and the love of God in a larger measure than any
> persons I know. Creep in among these, in spite of dirt, and a

hundred disgusting circumstances; and thus put off the gentlewoman.

—from a letter to "A Member of the Society," February 7, 1776

If all our associations are with the wealthy or well respected, how far we are from the practice of both Jesus and Wesley? Think for a minute. Who are your poor friends? To whom do you have regular encounters with those not of your own background? It's nice to send money to charities that benefit the poor, but it's much more Christlike to *know* the poor.

How is this done? There are ministries to the poor in your town that need volunteers, prayers, and donations. Every Christian must do what he or she can to "remember the poor." And that will mean going to them, not waiting for them to come to us.

I love the poor. In many of them I find pure genuine grace, unmixed with paint, folly, and affectation.

—from a letter, 1757

70

Without Worry

*Be anxious for nothing, but in everything by prayer and supplication,
with thanksgiving, let your requests be made known to God; and the
peace of God, which surpasses all understanding, will guard your
hearts and minds through Christ Jesus.*

—Philippians 4:6–7

The secret to the sheer energy John Wesley possessed was given in his journal entry for June 28, 1776, when he wrote,

I am 73 and far abler to preach than when I was three and twenty. What natural means has God used to produce so wonderful an effect?

1. Continual exercising and traveling about 400 miles a year.

2. Constant rising at 4 a.m.

3. The ability, if ever I want, to sleep immediately.

4. The never losing of a night's sleep in my life.

5. Two violent fevers and two deep consumptions. These, it is true, were rough medicines, but they were of admirable service, causing my flesh to come again as the flesh of a little child.

Then, almost as an afterthought, Wesley concludes with, "May I add lastly, evenness of temper? I feel and grieve, but by the grace of God, I fret at nothing."

Evenness of temper? Fretting at nothing?

Yes, John Wesley refused to worry. And he refused to become irate about anything. Simply put, he was unwilling that any negative emotion would rule his behavior. This trait was especially apparent during the many attacks upon his character and violence directed against him bodily. In case after case, he rose to the occasion by refusing to allow adverse circumstances to alter his mood. He would not fret. He would not return anger for anger.

Fretting, worry, and anxiety are the hallmarks of unbelief. A person who has cast their life fully on God, without reserve, may be *tempted* to fret—but they overcome it. They remind themselves that God is in control. What, then, can worrying do? Jesus reminded us of this when He asked, "Which of you by worrying can add one cubit to his stature?" (Matt. 6:27).

Worrying accomplishes nothing. Don't murmur about your present lot. Don't worry about your future. Cast all your cares on Him. Every one of them.

I dare no more murmur than I dare swear.

—from a letter

71

Living by Grace

In Him we have redemption through His blood, the forgiveness
of sins, according to the riches of His grace . . .

—Ephesians 1:7

The *riches* of His grace! How prone we are to think that our sin may exhaust God's grace towards us. Impossible! The grace of God can *never* be depleted. And best of all, this grace is *free!*

> [Grace] is free in all to whom it is given. It does not depend on any power or merit in man; no, not in any degree, neither in whole, nor in part. It does not in anywise depend either on the good works or righteousness of the receiver; not on anything he has done, or anything he is. It does not depend on his endeavors. It does not depend on his good tempers, or good desires, or good purposes and intentions; for all these flow from the free grace of God; they are the streams only, not the fountain. They are the fruits of free grace, and not the root. They are not the cause, but the effects of it. Whatsoever good is in man, or is done by man, God is the author and doer of it. Thus is His grace free in all; that is, no way depending on any power or merit in man, but on God

alone, who freely gave us His own Son, and "with Him freely giveth us all things."

—from "Free Grace," Sermon 128

What then, does this inexhaustible supply of grace depend on? Two things: the character of God, and our faith in appropriating all the grace necessary for life. As John Wesley said, grace is the source and faith is the condition of salvation. And this grace is not exhaustible. In a letter to one of his correspondents, Miss March, Wesley wrote, "To use the grace we have, and now to expect all we want is the grand secret." We must expect that grace will meet our every need of it.

All God's grace stands ready for each of today. We have only to look up and receive it by faith.

Look up, and receive a fresh supply of Grace!

—from a letter to Mrs. Moon, March 2, 1773

72

Busyness

As your days, so shall your strength be.

—Deuteronomy 33:25

John Wesley learned a great secret: to believe God for all the energy and sustenance required for the day ahead. Do not worry about what may happen tomorrow. Don't be drained by what happened yesterday. And watch out for our natural tendency to seek idleness. Wesley accomplished in one lifetime more than what most any other ten men would struggle to accomplish. Consider these insights to accomplishment from Wesley:

- Leisure and I have taken leave of one another.

- I propose to be busy as long as I live, if my health is so long indulged to me.

- It is impossible that an idle man can be a good man, sloth being inconsistent with religion.

- Without industry we are neither fit for this world nor for the world to come.

- Never be unemployed a moment. Never be triflingly employed. Never while away time.

Now, none of us are called to be John Wesley. There was only one of that great man, and he did his work and finished his race. Though our work is not his, it *is* our work. We have an assignment from God, given to us in eternity past. And we also have the necessary strength to do it *all*. We just do it one day at a time, believing God for the power to do that one day's necessary work. If we receive by faith the strength necessary for today, we will always have great things to do.

Wherever the work of our Lord is to be carried on, that is my place for today. And we live only for today. It is not our part to take thought for tomorrow.

—from a letter to Mrs. Marston, December 14, 1770

73

Embracing Change

Moab has been at ease from his youth;
He has settled on his dregs,
And has not been emptied from vessel to vessel,
Nor has he gone into captivity.
Therefore his taste remained in him,
And his scent has not changed.

—Jeremiah 48:11

John Wesley once wrote in a letter, "I know, were I myself to preach one whole year in one place, I should preach both myself and most of my congregation asleep. Nor can I believe it was ever the will of our Lord that any congregation should have one teacher only."

For that reason, Wesley was constantly on the move, rarely staying in one place long. As a result, by the end of his life he had traveled nearly a quarter of a million miles and preached at least forty-two thousand sermons.

Many of us seem to have a resistance to change. Sometimes God has to get our attention by bringing changes through unexpected circumstances or opportunities.

But we must always be careful of trying to engineer change on our own. Wesley's increasing desire to be married led him into a disastrous marriage. That was one change he would have done better without. We, too, often get ourselves in hot water by prodding the Lord to change things in our life, when we really should just be prayerful and watching for His opportunities.

Don't force change. But don't resist it either. If God's in it, it will be a change for the better.

When confronted with complaints about his departure from the Anglican Church's decorum with his "field preaching" and "class-meetings," Wesley replied this way:

> We are always open to instruction, willing to be wiser every day than we were before, and to change whatever we can change for the better.
>
> —from "A Plain Account of the People Called Methodists"

74

Following the Bible

Your word is a lamp to my feet
And a light to my path.
—Psalm 119:105

In his sermon "An Appeal to Men of Reason and Religion," Wesley says,

"I am a spirit come from God and returning to God. . . . I want to know one thing: the way to heaven. . . . God Himself has condescended to teach me the way. . . . He has written it down in a book. O give me that book! At any price, give me the book of God! I have it: here is knowledge enough for me. Let me be *homo unius libri* (a man of one book). Here then I am, far from the busy ways of men. I sit down alone. Only God is here. In His presence I open, I read His book; for this end, to find the way to Heaven."

Not only did Wesley find the way to heaven in the Bible, but he found the measure for daily living here on earth. He feasted on the Word of God and drew enough riches from it to produce forty-two thousand sermons, plus his many volumes of books illuminating the truths of Scripture, over the course of half a century.

Does the Bible occupy that central place in our life that it held in Wesley's? Do we feed on it as on manna from heaven? This was Wesley's way, and it is our way, if we are Christians.

The Word of God is a lamp for our feet. It gives us our bearing, our direction.

Today, it has become commonplace to relegate the Bible to a lesser place, while elevating our educated human reason, science, technology, or even our human intuition.

All of these tools are useful, but Wesley would beg us to keep their benefits in perspective. Without a firm grounding in the Bible, we can easily skid off the right path, even with the best of all other resources.

Live from the Bible. Make it your cornerstone. Follow it in all things.

My ground is the Bible. Yes, I am a Bible bigot. I follow it in all things, both great and small.

—from John Wesley's journal, June 5, 1766

75

Holiness Equals Happiness

*The thief does not come except to steal, and to kill, and to
destroy. I have come that they may have life, and that
they may have it more abundantly.*

—John 10:10

Holiness has gotten a bad rap. The life of holiness signals to
many a life of deprivation, a somberness that repels joy. But
nothing could be further from the truth. The true Christian life is the
joyful life—the abundant life—as Jesus stated was His reason for
coming. An abundant life is a life full of Jesus Christ. He lives in us,
producing all the things we used to seek when we were in the world:
peace, happiness, power, and yes, holiness. He does, after all, live
within us through the power of the *Holy* Spirit.

John Wesley hungered after personal holiness. And here's why:

And till their eye is single they are as far remote from happiness
as from holiness. They may now and then have agreeable
dreams, from Wealth, honor, pleasure, or what else This
short-enduring world can give: But none of these can satisfy
the appetite of an immortal soul. Nay, all of them together
cannot give rest, which is the lowest ingredient of happiness,
to a never-dying spirit, which God created for the enjoyment

of himself. The hungry soul, like the busy bee, wanders from flower to flower; but it goes off from each, with an abortive hope, and a deluded expectation.

—from "On the Single Eye," Sermon 118

As the more holy we are upon the earth the more happy we must be (seeing there is an inseparable connection between holiness and happiness).

—from "God's Love to Fallen Man"

Wesley saw that inevitable link between holiness and happiness. He saw that the pursuit of holiness was, in fact, the essence of life—and of Christianity. As he put it, "Repentance is the porch to religion, faith is the door to religion and the essence of religion is holiness."

And so it is. A fierce hunger for God and His holiness, a love for Christ that dwarfs all other claims on our affections—this is the way to happiness.

Holiness *is* happiness. And holiness is rooted in love.

But we must love God before we can be holy at all; this being the root of all holiness.

—from "The Witness of the Spirit"

76

The Accepted Time

*But we all, with unveiled face, beholding as in a mirror the glory of
the Lord, are being transformed into the same image from glory
to glory, just as by the Spirit of the Lord.*

—2 Corinthians 3:18

We are so apt to expect spiritual maturity overnight. We want
patience and we want it *now*. But do we want to be a shallow
rooted, fast-growing poplar tree or a sturdy, slow-growing oak tree?

Even so, Wesley notes that we shouldn't seek to grow slowly, but
instead, look for God's working in our lives every day, every hour,
every moment.

Everyone, though born of God in an instant, yea, and sanctified in an instant, yet undoubtedly grows by slow degrees,
both after the former and the latter change. But it does not follow from thence, that there must be a considerable tract of
time between the one and the other. A year or a month is the
same with God as a thousand. If He wills, to do is present
with Him: much less is there any necessity for much suffering: God can do His work by pleasure as well as by pain. It
is, therefore, undoubtedly our duty to pray and look for full
salvation every day, every hour, every moment, without waiting

till we have either done or suffered more. Why should not *this* be the accepted time?

—from a letter to Miss March, June 27, 1760

Are you not where you wish to be spiritually? Rather than looking to the future for what may happen then, why not look at what He is doing *now*?

Yes, today, God is at work in you. Let *today* be the accepted time for His work in you.

Redeem the time. Catch the golden moments as they fly.

—from a letter to his wife, July 12, 1760

77

Reaching the Lost

*Go out into the highways and hedges, and compel them
to come in, that my house may be filled.*

—Luke 14:23

*I*t was a major turnabout for John Wesley to admit that his old friend George Whitefield had been right about the practicality of open-field preaching. And as soon as he began to follow Whitefield's lead, the opposition he had voiced followed him from the mouths of others.

But what was it that caused Wesley to have such a marked change of mind? The answer is simple: Wesley wanted to reach the lost with the gospel. He knew the men and women he most wanted to preach to would never set foot in the church and, if they had, they would likely have been looked at with suspicion by the set-in-their-ways traditionalists. In his very direct way, Wesley rebuked his opposition:

> I wonder at those who still talk so loudly of the indecency of field preaching. The highest indecency is in St. Paul's Church, where a considerable part of the congregation are asleep, or talking, or looking about, not minding a word the preacher says.
>
> On the other hand, there is the highest decency in a churchyard or field, when the whole congregation behave and

look as if they saw the Judge of all, and heard Him speaking from heaven.

—from John Wesley's journal, 1759

Have we not used [outdoor preaching] too sparingly? It seems we have:

1. Because our call is to save that which is lost. Now we cannot expect them to come to *us*. Therefore we should go and seek *them*.

2. Because we are particularly called by "going into the highways and hedges," which none else will do, "to compel them to come in."

3. Because that reason against it is not good: "The [church] house will hold all that come." The house may hold that come to the house; but not all that would come to the field.

—from the Minutes of Conference, Wesley's Works, volume 3

What might be the equivalent of open air preaching in your life? Are there ways you can be more effective in living your faith or in reaching the lost?

Be willing to be innovative. Ask God to do a "new thing" in your life and in your church. It can change everything.

I would observe every punctilio of order, except when the salvation of souls is at stake. Then I prefer the end to the means.

—from a letter to George Downing, April 6, 1761

78

The Plain
Old Faith

Beloved, while I was very diligent to write to you concerning our common salvation, I found it necessary to write to you exhorting you to contend earnestly for the faith which was once for all delivered to the saints.

—Jude 3

O beware of all those teachers of lies, who would palm [error] upon you for Christianity! Regard them not, although they should come unto you with all the deceivableness of unrighteousness; with all smoothness of language, all decency, yea, beauty and elegance of expression, all professions of earnest good will to you, and reverence for the Holy Scriptures.

—from "Original Sin," Sermon 44

False teachers have been with us from the beginning. They are those who pervert the gospel to their ends. Wesley had no time for such wolves who would lead the sheep astray.

The faith in Christ that John Wesley preached is the same faith that the Bible portrays and that has been enjoyed by Christians for two thousand years. It's not complicated, really. Often, we make it seem harder than it is.

John Wesley learned this lesson the hard way. Early in his ministry he seriously doubted that any lost soul could be saved outside of the four walls of the church building. If someone came to faith in an open field, as was happening with the blossoming ministry of George Whitefield, Wesley thought the conversion dubious at best.

Of course, it was not long after that Wesley himself took the gospel message to the fields in a similar fashion as Whitefield. Yes, he discovered, the simple New Testament faith is still true, no matter the setting.

Our faith in Christ is that *old* faith "which was once delivered to the saints" (Jude 3). But it's also the new wine that Jesus proclaimed that can never really be old.

Many modern-day skeptics or revilers of Christianity want to move on, philosophically. They want to find truth that fits the twenty-first century—a faith that is tailor-made to our changing lifestyle. But in rejecting or adjusting Christian truth to their own needs, they overlook the most comfortable and enduring truth to be found on earth. The simple message that says, "Jesus loves me. This I know, for the Bible tells me so."

That's the old faith. And yet it's always new to those who believe, and always the cure to our terminal disease of sin.

Keep to the plain old faith, "once delivered to the saints," and delivered by the Spirit of God to our hearts. Know your disease! Know your cure!

—from "Original Sin"

79

Miracles

And whatever things you ask in prayer, believing, you will receive.

—Matthew 21:22

As we live our lives in this natural world, we tend to forget that our God is a God who transcends the natural, who performs miracles.

John Wesley trusted a supernatural God. In his long life, a fortune passed through his hands. But Wesley never saw his income as something he must seek or keep for a rainy day. *God* supplied it.

As for his health, Wesley wrote a bestselling book on health matters. It sold many copies in his lifetime and was still in print after his death. But even as he took good care of himself, He relied on a supernatural God to be the source of his health.

Consider the following entries from his journal:

In the evening [of November 12, 1746], at the Chapel my teeth pained me much. In coming home Mr. Spear gave me an account of the rupture he had had for some years, which after the most eminent physicians had declared it incurable was perfectly cured in a moment. I prayed, with submission to the will of God. My pain ceased, and returned no more.

Or how about asking God to miraculously change the weather? For John Wesley, it was the natural thing to do. In June of 1750, Wesley sailed from Ireland to England and encountered strong shifting winds that rocked the boat, so much so that the captain of the ship was worried, knowing "the danger of beating about, when it was pitch-dark, among these rocks and sands."

"But does not God hear the prayer?" Wesley records that he and a companion prayed, and "in a very few moments the wind was small, the sea fell, and the clouds dispersed." The ship docked in peace and God was given the glory.

On another occasion, Wesley's horse went lame far from help. Wesley prayed and "immediately the horse's lameness was gone."

What is there in your life that needs a miracle from God? Is it your finances? Your health? Your marriage or family? Doubts or fears?

No matter what it is that you feel is beyond your control, God can supply your need, either through natural means or supernatural means, whichever He deems best.

Don't be afraid to ask. He's your father, and He delights to give to His children.

"What! You expect miracles then?" Certainly I do, if I believe the Bible: For the Bible teaches me, that God hears and answers prayer: But every answer to prayer is, properly, a miracle.

—from "On Divine Providence"

Christian Unity

*I, therefore, the prisoner of the Lord, beseech you to walk worthy of
the calling with which you were called, with all lowliness, gentleness,
with longsuffering, bearing with one another in love, endeavoring
to keep the unity of the Spirit in the bond of peace.*

—Ephesians 4:1–3

John Wesley never intended for his societies to become a denomination.
He thought that he could bring new life to the established Anglican
Church and attempted to do so at every turn. But it just wasn't possible.
The traditionalists rebuffed him, and his followers would have nothing
to do with the dead church many of them had come out of.

In a ministry as long and as widespread as Wesley's, there was
also the likelihood of division among those in the ranks. And sure
enough, every so often—much to Wesley's heartbreak—some would
split off, often into the Calvinist groups that also flourished during
this time.

A good example of Wesley's attitude toward those who were on
the opposite side of a doctrinal dispute can be found in his relationship to the great evangelist, George Whitefield. The two men had
been friends since young adulthood.

But when Whitefield embraced Calvinism, the men grew apart.
So much so that Whitefield openly denounced Wesley and published
a pamphlet condemning him.

Although Wesley was deeply disappointed, he took it in stride and when asked, "Do you intend to reply to Mr. Whitefield's pamphlet?" he replied, "Sir, you may read Whitefield against Wesley, but you shall never read Wesley against Whitefield."

And no one ever did.

Eventually Wesley and Whitefield came to a truce regarding their differences—an outcome that could not have happened had Wesley not refused to side against his accuser. His sentiments on unity among Christians were well expressed in his sermon, "Of the Church," in which he wrote,

> The true members of the Church of Christ "endeavour," with all possible diligence, with all care and pains, with unwearied patience, (and all will be little enough) to "keep the unity of the Spirit in the bond of peace;" to preserve inviolate the same spirit of lowliness and meekness, of longsuffering, mutual forbearance, and love; and all these cemented and knit together by that sacred tie,—the peace of God filling the heart. Thus only can we be and continue living members of that Church which is the body of Christ.
>
> —from "Of the Church"

The body of Christ is *one* body. We are brothers and sisters in Christ. Nothing must divide us.

I love good men of every church.

—from John Wesley's journal, June 5, 1766

Higher or Lower Christians?

And yet I show you a more excellent way.

—1 Corinthians 12:31

From long experience and observation, I am inclined to think that whoever finds redemption in the blood of Jesus—whoever is justified—has the choice of walking in the higher or the lower path.

I believe the Holy Spirit at that time sets before him the "more excellent way," and incites him to walk therein—to choose the narrowest path in the narrow way—to aspire after the heights and depths of holiness—after the entire image of God.

But if he does not accept this offer, he insensibly declines into the lower order of Christians; he still goes on in what may be called a good way, serving God in his degree, and finds mercy in the close of life through the blood of the covenant.

—from "The More Excellent Way"

Is there a limit to how deep we can go as Christians? If so, who determines our maximum depth? For John Wesley, it was up to each

Christian to continue following God, ever deeper, ever farther along on the solitary path, "the more excellent way," the narrower path of love and service.

At many points along the wider path, we see an entryway to the narrower path and the invitation to forsake the well-worn path for the thornier, narrower path. Which shall we take?

If we were to ask Wesley, "Have you any regrets for choosing the narrower path?" what do you suppose his answer would be? In fact, can you think of one Christian anywhere who has taken the narrower path and found it full of regrets? On the other hand, haven't we known wider-path Christians who, at the end of the journey, regretted they had ignored the lesser path?

Let's decide that we will not be one of them. Let's choose the narrower path. The signpost is there, pointing our way today. Which will we take?

Who then is a wise man, and endued with knowledge among you? Let him resolve this day, this hour, this moment, the Lord assisting him, to choose in all the preceding particulars the "more excellent way:" And let him steadily keep it, both with regard to sleep, prayer, work, food, conversation, and diversions; and particularly with regard to the employment of that important talent, money.

—from "The More Excellent Way"

82

Societies

We know what real love is because Christ gave up his life for us.
And so we also ought to give up our lives for our
Christian brothers and sisters.

—1 John 3:16, NLT

When John Wesley returned to England from his failed American mission, he noted what happened to his old friend George Whitefield in the ensuing years. Whitefield, like Wesley, drew huge crowds and many were saved, but there was something critical missing, and Wesley saw what it was. Here's his report:

They did repent and believe the gospel. And by his ministry a line of communication was formed, quite from Georgia to New-England.

But the last journey he made, he acknowledged to some of his friends, that he had much sorrow and heaviness in his heart, on account of multitudes who for a time ran well, but afterwards "drew back unto perdition. . . ."

. . . Those who were more or less affected by Mr. Whitefield's preaching had no discipline at all. They had no shadow of discipline; nothing of the kind. They were formed into no societies: They had no Christian connection with each other, nor were ever taught to watch over each other's souls. So that if any fell into lukewarmness, or even into sin, he had none to lift him up: He might fall lower and lower, yea, into hell, if he would, for who regarded it?

John Wesley found a remedy to the problem of the Whitefield converts who were falling away:

Two of our Preachers willingly offered themselves to go to America. They laboured first in Philadelphia and New York; afterwards in many other places: And everywhere God was eminently with them, and gave them to see much fruit of their labour. What was wanting before was now supplied: Those who were desirous to save their souls were no longer a rope of sand, but clave to one another, and began to watch over each other in love. Societies were formed, and Christian discipline introduced in all its branches.

The work of God then not only spread wider, particularly in North Carolina, Maryland, Virginia, Pennsylvania, and the Jerseys, but sunk abundantly deeper than ever it had done before.

—from "The Late Work of God in North America"

There is no one lonelier than the troubled Christian who has no one to help him through deep waters. One role of the church is to express the love of Christ toward other believers in practical ways. When someone hurts, we *are* to be our brother's keeper. Let me ask you: is there someone who watches diligently over your soul? Do they know your deepest hurts? Your greatest victories? And then, let's turn the question around: are *you* there for your brothers and sisters in Christ? Are you "connected together" effectively?

You may be the answer to the prayes of someone you know. Build relationships with other believers and watch the church grow stronger.

83

The Gift of Time

See then that you walk circumspectly, not as fools but as wise,
redeeming the time, because the days are evil.

—Ephesians 5:15–16

John Wesley was scrupulous about time. Never one to be late or to waste time, he strongly resented it when others weren't punctual. Time represented life. It was something of high value to Wesley—and it should be to us as well.

On one occasion, when a man was ten minutes late for a meeting, Wesley said sharply, "I have lost ten minutes forever!"

On another occasion, when told he didn't need to be in a hurry, Wesley retorted, "A hurry? No, I have no time to be in a hurry."

Wesley was a man of order. He loathed loose ends. Part of his success as a man of God was due to his ability to manage himself and others. In his eighty-seven years, Wesley wasted no time. He traveled a quarter-million miles on horseback, preached over forty thousand sermons, and wrote or edited four hundred books and tracts.

How do we measure up in the area of "redeeming the time?" We all have only a few years in which to fulfill God's plan for our life. Let's learn to live without hurriedness, but appreciating the commodity of time as if it were gold. For it *is* gold that cannot be replaced.

Guard your time today.

Though I am always in haste, I am never in a hurry.

—from a letter, December 10, 1777

84

Renewal

For you were bought at a price; therefore glorify God in
your body and in your spirit, which are God's.

—1 Corinthians 6:20

I n 1780 John Wesley wrote a pamphlet on "Directions for Renewing our Covenant with God." His thought was that from time to time, believers need to reaffirm their covenant of faith with God. Typically, this has become an annual service at many Methodist churches, often part of the New Year's Celebration. But in Wesley's mind, it can be done anytime.

Part of the renewal is a beautiful prayer of surrender:

I am no longer my own, but yours. Put me to what you will, rank me with whom you will; put me to doing, put me to suffering; let me be employed for you or laid aside for you, exalted for you or brought low for you; let me be full, let me be empty; let me have all things, let me have nothing; I freely and heartily yield all things to your pleasure and disposal.

And now, O glorious and blessed God, Father, Son, and Holy Spirit, you are mine, and I am yours. So be it. And the Covenant which I have made on earth, let it be ratified in heaven.

It's not easy to include in our prayers, "put me to suffering," "let me be empty," or "let me have nothing." And yet the surrendered soul can truly leave the choosing to God of how He will use His own.

That was certainly true of John Wesley. As a young man, he would have gladly lived the simple life of a village Anglican priest, as his beloved father had done. Such would have made for a contented John Wesley—except for one thing. When God took possession of John Wesley, contentedness was forever redefined as being used by God as He sees fit.

Sometimes life doesn't work out the way we expect. We might become discouraged, unexpected circumstances change our destiny, illness may strike, and yet such a time of questioning is the perfect time to renew our covenant with God.

Yes, He can be trusted for the outcome.

Live a surrendered life today. What you offer to God, He gladly receives.

The times of renewing our covenant with God, should be times of rejoicing. It is an honour and happiness to be in bonds with God. And the closer, the better.

—from *Explanatory Notes on the Old Testament,* 2 Chronicles 15

Being Right

Happy is the man who finds wisdom,
And the man who gains understanding;
For her proceeds are better than the profits of silver,
And her gain than fine gold.

—Proverbs 3:13–14

When I was young I was sure of everything; in a few years, having been mistaken a thousand times, I was not half so sure of most things as I was before; at present, I am hardly sure of anything but what God has revealed to me.

—*London Magazine*, 1765

We have all been mistaken a thousand times—possibly in the past week. John Wesley was quick to admit his errors—and that there were many. That takes a transparency rarely found in leadership these days.

Part of godly wisdom is to know when you've been wrong and be willing to change your mind. And when we don't know the right way, we can always ask God for wisdom.

Sometimes, though, we're slow to ask God for wisdom. And yet, which of us who are parents would not be happy to have our child ask us to help them be wise? Which of us doesn't want a child that values truth above error?

Most of John Wesley's prolific writing and speaking was birthed out an insatiable desire to know the truth and to preach the truth to others. But even further, Wesley's goal was to have a heart that could bear the truth. Like most of us, Wesley found it hard to change, but if convinced of a matter, he *would* change.

One notable example stands out in Wesley's life.

On his missionary trip to the colony of Georgia in the new land of America, Wesley, as yet unregenerated, noticed the calm with which the several Moravian passengers withstood the violent storms that tossed the ship around. *How could they be so undisturbed?* Wesley wondered. Eventually, on his return to England, after his dismal failure in Georgia, Wesley met the Moravian leader, Peter Bohler, who gave him a hearing. Upon discerning Wesley's spiritual emptiness, Bohler said, "My brother, that philosophy of yours must be purged away!" The next time they met, Wesley admitted, "I am clearly convinced of unbelief—of the want of that faith whereby alone we are saved." Not long after, Wesley enjoyed his famous Aldersgate conversion experience all because he, a learned clergyman, was willing to be *wrong*. He was willing to surrender a long held misunderstanding about the nature of God and believe the truth about God.

Lord, deliver us from our desperate need to be *right* all the time. Give us the grace to *change* our foolish orthodoxies at Your command.

A man may be orthodox in every point; he may not only espouse right opinions, but zealously defend them against all opposers. . . . He may be almost as orthodox—as the devil.

—from "The Way of the Kingdom," Sermon 7

86

Worldliness

*Do not love the world or the things in the world. If anyone
loves the world, the love of the Father is not in him.*

—1 John 2:15

ow to avoid worldliness? Some Christian movements have
taken the bold step of adopting a form of dress or way of
cutting their hair as a badge of their separation from the world. In fact,
John Wesley almost regretted that he had not been more severe in this
regard:

> I am distressed. I know not what to do. I see what I might
> have done once.
>
> I might have said peremptorily and expressly, "Here I am:
> I and my Bible. I will not, I dare not vary from this book,
> either in great things or small. I have no power to dispense
> with one jot or tittle of what is contained therein. I am deter-
> mined to be a Bible Christian, not almost, but altogether.
>
> Who will meet me on this ground? Join me on this, or not
> at all." With regard to dress in particular, I might have been as
> firm (and I now see it would have been far better) as either the
> people called Quakers, or the Moravian brethren;—I might

have said, "This is our manner of dress, which we know is both Scriptural and rational. If you join us, you are to dress as we do; but you need not join us unless you please."

But, alas! the time is now past; and what I can do now, I cannot tell.

—from "Causes of Inefficacy of Christianity"

In his sermon "On Dress," Wesley frankly said, "Let me see, before I die, a Methodist congregation, full as plain dressed as a Quaker congregation."

Wesley worried about worldliness and thought that plain dressing might solve the problem. But for many Christians, worldliness isn't about dress; it's about what entices our heart away from God. In fact, Wesley defined *worldliness* as anything that lessened our love for God. For each of us, the answer may be different.

So guard your heart. Don't allow your spiritual life to become eroded through compromise.

Search us, O LORD, and prove us; try our reins and our heart. Look well if there be any way of wickedness in us, and lead us in the way everlasting. Let thy favor be better to us than life itself; that so in all things we may assure our hearts before thee, and feel the sense of thy acceptance of us, and—that joy which the world cannot give.

—from "Prayers for Families"

87

A Second Wind

And I say to the rest of you, dear brothers and sisters,
never get tired of doing good.

—2 Thessalonians 3:13, NLT

During his eighty-seven years of ministry, John Wesley never seemed to grow weary. In fact, it was his devotion to the work God had given him that seemed to energize him. In his later years, he could work rings around men half his age. It is as if he was immortal until his work in this life was finished. Is it possible that you, too, are immortal until your work here is complete?

Sometimes we grow weary in the day-to-day fulfillment of our duties. And yet, like Wesley, the Spirit of God can actually renew our strength as we work. There were times when Wesley was drained in body or ill—but he pushed on and gained strength through being faithful to the task at hand. His journal entry for May 10, 1741, is a remarkable testimony of God's empowerment of our weak bodies:

> While I was speaking, my pain vanished, the fever left me, my bodily strength returned and for many weeks I felt neither weakness nor pain. Unto thee, O Lord, do I give thanks.

On another occasion, Wesley records:

But God renewed my strength, so that I felt less and pain and weariness every hour. I had a solemn and delightful ride to Keswick, having my mind stayed on God.

—from John Wesley's journal, September 26, 1749

We can get a second wind by having our mind stayed on God. From that second wind can come some of our greatest triumphs. That's the way it was for John Wesley, whose latter half of ministry was equal to or greater than the first half.

Thou art never weary, O Lord, of doing us good. Let us never be weary of doing thee service. Let us take pleasure in thy service and abound in thy work and in thy love and praise evermore. Fill up all that is wanting, reform whatever is amiss in us, perfect the thing that concerns us, and let the witness of thy pardoning love ever abide in all our hearts.

—from "Prayers for Families"

88

Your Work

*Who then is Paul, and who is Apollos, but ministers through whom
you believed, as the Lord gave to each one? I planted, Apollos watered,
but God gave the increase. So then neither he who plants is anything,
nor he who waters, but God who gives the increase. Now he who
plants and he who waters are one, and each one will receive his
own reward according to his own labor.*

—1 Corinthians 3:5–8

[Y]ou will frequently see little fruit of all your labor.
But leave that with Him. The success is His. The
work only is yours.

—from a letter to Mary Bishop, November 4, 1772

We look back at the whole of John Wesley's life and we see a life
that changed the world. But we have the perspective of history. We
have the advantage of time. We can see the whole of the life that
Wesley lived. But in so doing, we may miss the many failures, set-
backs, false steps, and circumstances beyond Wesley's control that
were the disappointments of his life.

Life is full of disappointments. We work hard and see little
results and think that we've failed. The only real failure, though, is
to walk away from the work. The *work* is yours; the *results* are up
to God.

God looks for faithfulness in His people, those who will put their hands to the plow and not look back at the furrow behind them. Keep your eye fixed only on the mark at the end of the row: Jesus. And keep the furrow ahead of you straight. That's all you can ever do—and it is enough.

God grant that I may never live to be useless.

—from John Wesley's journal, July 13, 1764

89

Even in Death

For to me, to live is Christ, and to die is gain.

—Philippians 1:21

John Wesley was a hero in death, as in life. In his will, he made several stipulations regarding his funeral and the disposition of his meager belongings. Here are a few of the most notable provisions:

- His body was to be buried in cheap material, nothing costly was to be wasted on his corpse.

- "Whatever remains in my bureau and pockets at my decease," he directed, was to be equally divided among four poor itinerants, whom he named.

- "I give six pounds to be divided among the six poor men, named by the Assistant, who shall carry my body to the grave."

- "I particularly desire there may be no hearse, no coach, no escutcheon, no pomp, except the tears of them that loved me, and are following me to Abraham's bosom."

- "I give the books, furniture, and whatever else belongs to me in the three houses at Kingswood, in trust to [those] still employed in teaching and maintaining the children of poor Traveling Preachers."

Every Christian has a home not made with human hands—a home reserved for him or her in heaven. For many long decades, John Wesley looked longingly toward that day. When it finally arrived, he was joyous—and ready.

Too often we say we long for heaven, but not just yet. We have so much we want to do, so much we want to experience. But if, in God's providence, we should be called home sooner than we would have liked, may we each leave behind the earth with the grace and simplicity of the man, John Wesley.

In the Name of God, Amen.

—the opening lines of John Wesley's Last Will and Testament

90

The Work of God Goes On

*For we are His workmanship, created in Christ Jesus for
good works, which God prepared beforehand
that we should walk in them.*

—Ephesians 2:10

The realization that every Christian has been created to do a special work, designed by God just for them, is life changing. We, like Wesley, and every other great man and woman of God, will find our purpose and fulfillment in doing that for which we were created. It was constantly John Wesley's testimony that he *loved* his calling. God gifted him with the energy, the insight, and the vision to accomplish great things.

Wesley's journal is remarkable in recalling his last years. At age seventy he declared he felt "refreshed with new wine." Seven years later he would proclaim that he felt the same as he did at age twenty-eight. At age eighty he declared that he found no more infirmities in himself than when he was "in the flower of manhood." Two years later he would write, "It is now eleven years since have felt any such thing as weariness." At age eighty-five, he finally admitted to a decline in his agility and a weakening of his sight. Then, at age eighty-six he said, "I now find I grow old." And yet he was still preaching two sermons a day! Then, near the end, a year later he said, "I am now an old man, decayed from head to foot." With death approaching, he said, "Blessed be God! I do not slack my labors! I can preach and write still." And so he did. He preached his last sermon only a week before his death.

Shortly thereafter he was in bed, still rejoicing, proclaiming, "Christ is all! Christ is all!" His loving supporters were gathered about his bed near the end. He slept, then awoke with the words, "Pray and praise!"

He shook hands with all those present and beaming, wished each one, "Farewell!"

Then he exalted: "The best of all is, God is with us!"

After a brief pause, he waved his arm in triumph and repeated with joy, "The best of all is, God is with us!"

On Wednesday, March 2, 1791, the great man cried once again, "Farewell! The silver cord is loosed . . . the golden bowl is broken!" And John Wesley departed for his eternal home.

Yes, a man of God died—but the work of God goes on. It goes on in us. We put our hands to the plow and do what God has set before us, large or small.

And best of all, God is with us.

God buries his workmen, but carries on his work.

—engraved on the monument in Westminster Abbey
to the memory of John and Charles Wesley

Other Devotional Books
by Nick Harrison

Promises to Keep: Daily Devotions for Men Seeking Integrity

365 WWJD: Daily Answers to "What Would Jesus Do?"

His Victorious Indwelling

Magnificent Prayer

Survival Guide for New Dads: Two-Minute Devotions for Successful Fatherhood (with Steve Miller)